"I give him a high five!

...I've been working a three-day week from my home since 1971 and I suspect I'd have earned twice as much or more if I had read Doug's wondrous guide."

—Jay Conrad Levinson, Author, "Guerrilla Marketing" series of books
Over 14 million sold; now in 39 languages

"The Free Agent Marketing Guide *offers smart, practical advice on every single page. Whether you're just starting out, or whether you've been on your own for years, if you work for yourself, this book is essential reading."*

—Daniel H. Pink, Author, *Free Agent Nation*

"100% Fat Free! Jammed with useful resources that will pay off for anyone willing to work hard enough to become an overnight success."

—Seth Godin, Author, *Purple Cow*

"This is as concise and powerful a manual as any entrepreneur can ask for, covering virtually every aspect of marketing. It's a rich trove of revenue-generating ideas, many of which take only minutes to implement."

—Alan Weiss, Ph.D., Author, *Million Dollar Consulting*

"Whether you're a rookie or a veteran, The Free Agent Marketing Guide *provides a treasure trove of tips for thriving in a cut-throat marketing climate. It will come in handy again and again."*

—Maggie Jackson, author of *What's Happening to Home? Balancing Work, Life and Refuge in the Information Age*

"Short, sweet straightforward and smart! The Free Agent Marketing Guide *is a powerful collection of valuable nuggets for independent practitioners to grow their business in any economy."*

–Alex L. Goldfayn, The Technology Tailor
On-air Technology Expert, Fox News Chicago

"Doug Florzak has created the ultimate marketing guide for the Free Agent who wants to (needs to!) create the biggest bang for their marketing buck. It is so ripe with resources that implementing these savvy tips will be a breeze. These are new ideas for a new time and a new type of entrepreneur."

–Lee Welles/owner, MARS Fitness Services

"It is all here, everything a 'free agent' needs. Read it like a novel — because it reads well; Doug's enthusiasm comes through, providing a shot of encouragement along with his practical suggestions. Use it like a manual — pick a section that applies to your current situation and follow Doug's advice, step-by-step. Even if you don't get the sale the first time, you will learn something about yourself that you will use over and over."

–Derek Robe, independent marketing contractor

The Free Agent Marketing Guide

Other books in the Successful Independent series:

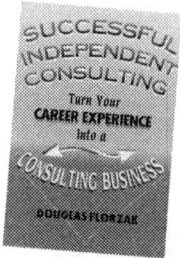

Successful Independent Consulting
Turn Your Career Experience
Into a Consulting Business
by Doug Florzak

(See the back of this book for ordering information)

The Free Agent Marketing Guide

100+
MARKETING TIPS
for Free Agents,
Independent Consultants,
and Freelancers

DOUGLAS FLORZAK

LOGICAL DIRECTIONS, INC.
Westmont, IL

First printing 2004

ISBN 0-9671565-0-5

LCCN 2003096276

ATTENTION CORPORATIONS, UNIVERSITIES, COLLEGES, AND PROFESSIONAL ORGANIZATIONS: Quantity discounts are available on bulk purchases of this book for educational purposes. Special books or book excerpts can also be created to fit specific needs. For information, please contact Logical Directions, Inc., PO Box 19, Westmont, Il 60559. E-mail publisher@LDIPub.com.

Acknowlegements

As with my first effort, *Successful Independent Consulting*, I could not complete this book without the help of family, friends, colleagues, and other free agents. I want to thank all the free agents who shared their "guerrilla marketing stories" with me. I particularly want to cite those whose stories are included in this book:

- Tom Anderson of Real Work Business Results, Inc.
- Joe Barranco of Century 21 Real Estate
- Jennifer Berkley of The Insight Advantage
- Nancy Michaels, author of *Off the Wall Marketing* and owner of Impression Impact
- Andrea Price of Andrea Price Project Management & Implementation
- Derek Robe, an independent marketing contractor
- Jim Salmons and Timlynn Babitsky of Sohodojo Inc.
- Lee Welles of MARS Fitness Services
- Chris Young of The Rainmaker Group

I also want to thank my editors Barbara Simmons, ELS, a Fellow of the Society for Technical Communication (STC) and Lane Kamps. I'm convinced they helped raise the quality of this book.

Finally, I want to thank my family and my wife, Laurie, for their support and encouragement. This includes a thank you to Jordan, my protégé for his support and youthful enthusiasm.

Contents

Introduction

"We are entering an era that's going to change the way almost everything is marketed to almost everybody."
— Seth Godin, author of *Unleashing the Ideavirus*. Quoted in *Fast Company* Magazine (April/May, 1998)

Whenever pollsters ask small-business owners their most challenging business task, "marketing" or "promoting their business" inevitably takes the top spot. Both large and small companies face the same problem. CEOs of billion-dollar companies as well as sole proprietors of one-person public relations firms lose sleep asking the same question, "How do I reach my customers and increase market share?"

While the problem is the same, the options differ. The CEO has more money, people, and resources to throw at marketing his or her company. The free agent has very little money, usually only himself or herself, and few resources. Free agents usually have to do everything themselves; thus they have to find time to fit marketing into a crammed schedule that includes delivering the service or product, developing new offerings, doing the books, collecting their money, and so on. As someone who has operated his own business for the past 12 years, I know the list is endless.

As if this wasn't challenging enough, the entire marketing environment is changing. In nature, an evolutionary symbiosis exists between predator and prey. Over millions of years, every advance by a predator has been countered by an offsetting defense by the prey. Similarly, as the marketing industry has refined the distribution of its message, the consuming public has improved its skills at avoiding it. For every marketing innovation, such as call centers, pop-up windows, and spam mail, consumers have countered with answering machines, anti-pop-up software, and Spam filters.

1

Even good, old-fashioned word of mouth is more difficult to get started. As Seth Godin points out in his book *Purple Cow: Transform Your Business by Being Remarkable*, "Because marketers have overwhelmed consumers with too much of everything, people are less likely to go out of their way to tell a friend about a product unless they're fairly optimistic that the friend will be glad to hear about it." In other words, the U.S. economy is the victim of its own success. As more product and service choices are made available, there is less and less time to filter through them, so consumers just tune most of them out.

Moreover, even global political strife is affecting marketing. The September 11 attacks and terrorism have changed how the mail is used. At one time, many marketing books suggested that it was a good technique to handwrite addresses, leave no return address, and put lots of stamps on a letter or package to make marketing mail stand out from mass mail. They might even suggest marking the letter or package "confidential." But, after the post-September 11 anthrax attacks, as demonstrated in huge posters at post offices, these are exactly the things that are flagged to identify a "suspicious package." Even before September 11, the Unabomber prompted the U.S. Postal Service to change the rules governing delivery of packages weighing more than one pound. The post office requires that any package weighing more than one pound be personally delivered to a post office employee.

How does a small-business owner market in this environment when even the "big guys" are struggling to get their value proposition across? The good news is that having a lot of money to spend on advertising does not necessarily guarantee success. Just ask the people behind New Coke, the Edsel, and any failed dot com. One advantage of not having a lot of money or resources is that it forces the small-business owner to focus. Numerous good, effective, low-cost techniques are available for the small-business owner who is willing to commit time and elbow grease. Although many of these techniques have been around a long time, I think Jay Conrad Levinson deserves a great deal of credit for bringing these concepts into the small-business consciousness. His "guerrilla marketing" books established an entire language for this marketing niche.

When the employer-employee relationship was the primary way businesses organized work, there was little incentive for an individual to "throw away" the perceived security of a steady paycheck for the risks of starting a business, particularly a solo business. There were fewer books on starting a business and fewer still on marketing for a small business. There were also fewer terms for this kind of person. Before it became mainstream, a person starting his or her own business might be called "self-employed," "contractor," "freelancer," "entrepreneur," or perhaps, simply "odd."

Since then, the way businesses organize work has changed dramatically, with an emphasis on "outsourcing." At the same time, many employees have asked themselves the same question about their business lives as they have about life in general, "Is this all there is?" An early observer of this new economic, technological, and social transformation is Daniel Pink, author of *Free Agent Nation: How Americas New Independent Workers are Transforming the Way We Live.* In his book, Pink describes a free agent as "simultaneously independent and connected to others." He estimates that there are 33 million free agents in the United States, constituting one in four workers. So there are more of us than ever, but we still have to find customers.

This book focuses on marketing for the free agent. Although most of the tips in this book are directed at the one-person business, many of them can also be used for larger, multiperson businesses with a free agent spirit. Among the 100+ marketing tips, most are very inexpensive or cost no money at all. Wherever possible, I include specific resources that will help you implement a particular marketing concept. Also, throughout the text are "in practice" profiles of free agents who successfully implemented particular techniques.

This book is not intended to be an all-encompassing guide. Not all these techniques will work for all types of businesses. Some techniques I've personally used, and other techniques I've seen colleagues use. Still other techniques I've uncovered through research but have not tried. More experienced free agents may scan the list of tips and ask, "Where's the discussion of a unique selling proposition (USP) and direct mail?" I avoid some common marketing concepts in this book because either I touched on the subject in a different way or I thought many other books covered the subject far better than I could. Some may conclude that many of these marketing ideas are obvious. However, rookie free agents might still benefit from these tips, and for veterans these techniques might stimulate a new spin on some old ideas.

As you read this book, note the marketing techniques you want to try. As the list becomes lengthy, you should think about prioritizing your efforts. In my book *Successful Independent Consulting: Turn Your Career Experience into a Con-*

sulting Business, I categorized marketing activities as either "active" or "passive." Active techniques require personal interaction. As such, they are "expensive" because even if they don't cost money, they require dedicated "face time." Examples are making cold calls, networking, giving seminars, and teaching. Passive marketing techniques sell your business in a way that doesn't require personal interaction. Examples include getting listings in directories (membership, yellow pages, who's who, and the like), developing a Web page, and writing articles.

Passive techniques require some upfront time to get started, but, when properly implemented, they continue to broadcast your message, "passing" leads through to you. Passive marketing techniques depend heavily on a "high profile" concept. With a high profile, your message hangs in the public arena where you hope it will "bump into" your target audience. Because of the lingering quality of passive marketing techniques, they typically represent the most efficient method for the one-person business short on time.

Another way to organize a marketing plan is to determine where each marketing idea falls in the cost/effort marketing matrix. An example of this matrix is shown below.

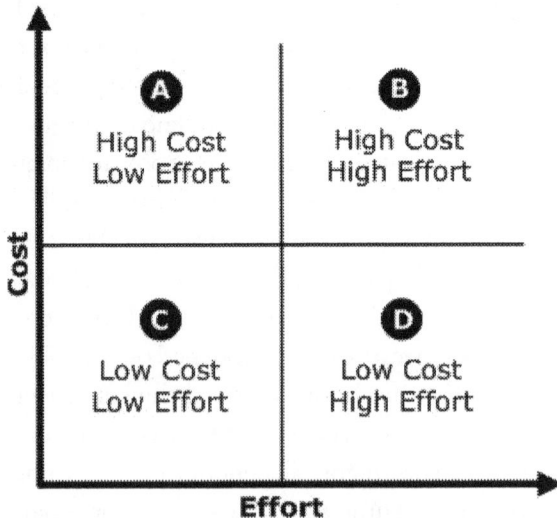

The Cost/Effort Marketing Matrix

This matrix helps you analyze the balance between effort and cost. Effort includes time, energy, and emotional commitment. Cost is the hard dollars that must be expended to implement the marketing idea. Together, cost and effort form the basis for calculating the return on investment (ROI). As you think about marketing ideas, try to determine where the idea fits into the matrix.

The matrix is divided into four quadrants. Marketing techniques that fit into quadrant A require more money but relatively little effort. An example of a marketing technique that falls into this quadrant is hiring a public relations firm. In this example, you are basically sacrificing money for time while delegating your marketing effort to someone else.

Quadrant B requires high cost and high effort. Marketing techniques that fall into this quadrant are the most risky, because a great deal of time and money is required. A marketing technique that could fall into this quadrant is producing and distributing a video about your business.

In contrast, the least risky techniques apply to quadrant C. These techniques require little effort and low or no cost. A technique that fits this area is registering your profile on a free agent job website such as FreeAgent.com or eLance.com.

Finally, in quadrant D more effort than money is expended. This is where you invest your "sweat equity." Writing a book (assuming it's not self-published) or writing an article for a trade magazine are examples of marketing techniques that qualify for this quadrant.

In addition to cost and effort, there is a third element to consider in using the matrix: ROI, which is the net result of a marketing effort translated into revenue (or loss) for the company. It's the difference between what the company got back (more customers, increased revenue) minus what was invested (money spent to implement the technique plus the value of your time and effort). I did not include ROI in the matrix itself because of the complexities of a three-dimensional array. However, after you peg a marketing technique to the matrix, consider the ROI. For example, even though quadrant B requires the most cost and effort, if you're convinced it will return 10 times its cost in customers and revenue, then it's probably worth it.

Of course pegging a marketing technique to the matrix is subjective. Different free agents may peg the same technique differently. Some free agents have the appropriate skills to reduce the effort, while others will struggle with the same technique. Some free agents will have more money for marketing than others. Also, many free agents will have different thresholds of what constitutes a "high cost." Nevertheless, the cost/effort marketing matrix provides a way to organize your marketing efforts.

The goal of this book is to stimulate marketing ideas. I hope that at least one idea will provide a fair ROI for your investment in this book. Even if you can't see a way to implement a particular tip, I hope it will at least get you thinking. As you read these marketing tips, analyze them, turn them upside down, and plug in different parameters. Then tape them to the wall, stand back, and see what you've got. In this way, you'll write your own Free Agent Marketing Guide.

Branding Your Image

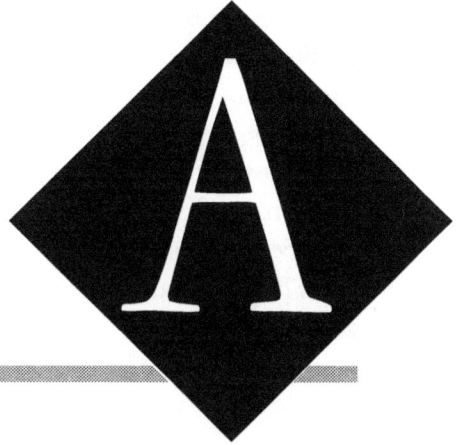

"My image is a statement of the symbols of the harsh, impersonal products and brash materialistic objects on which America is built today. It is a projection of everything that can be bought and sold, the practical but impermanent symbols that sustain us."

−Andy Warhol (1928−87), U.S. pop artist. "New Talent USA," in *Art in America*, vol. 50, no. 1 (New York, 1962).

Even if you are a one-person business, you have to think about your "brand." Branding is how you position your business identity so that it stands out from the crowd. Often free agents and small-business owners think that branding is a hugely expensive exercise only undertaken by the Nikes and Coca-Colas of the world, companies that can afford to hire fancy advertising agencies to establish their brand. The branding tactics of companies that seek an international mass market for their products may be appropriate for large, multi-national corporations. However, simple and far less expensive branding strategies are equally important for a one-person business with a much smaller target market. Branding for a free agent can be as simple as selecting an effective name or as elaborate as franchising the business.

1. Select an effective name

The first and most important decision for a business is selecting its name. In many circumstances, the business name has to stand on its own without the advantage of additional explanation from a brochure or business card. For example, the business name may be printed in a list of contributors for a charity or in a professional directory with no additional information. In these circumstances, ask yourself, "If that's all people see, can people find me?" and "Does my business name describe what I do?" An effective name is simple, easy to pronounce, and hard to confuse with other business names and communicates something about what you do and/or the benefits you provide your customers.

There are many sophisticated ways to create a name for a business. Linguists have identified some 600,000 morphemes (the smallest meaningful word unit) that can be combined for practically unlimited naming possibilities. Brand designers have used morphemes to create some very famous corporate names. For example, Sony is built on the morpheme "son," which means "sound." The name of the Acura automobile company is based on the morpheme "acu," which means "precisely" or "with care." There's even software that can help in selecting a name. However, you don't have to bend your mind in knots to come up with an effective name for your business.

The following are some questions to ask while creating your business name:

- How about your own name? The simplest and safest way to name your business is to base it on your own name. A business based on your own name is unlikely to infringe on another business name.

- Is the name being used by anyone else? If you decide not to use your own name, conduct a trademark search to ensure you don't infringe on someone else's business name.

- Is it easy to pronounce and spell? If you plan to do business internationally, consider whether a non-English-speaking client can handle your business name.

- How does it sound and print? Make sure the name does not accidentally rhyme with or sound like an embarrassing or negative word or phrase. Listen to how the name will sound on the phone or on the radio. See how it will look in print.

- Does it describe your business? Try to come up with a name that communicates what you do, such as "Jones Accounting Services."

- Does it communicate a benefit? Examples include jiffy, quick, affordable, executive, 24-hour, and so on.

- How does it sort? If most of your business will come from yellow page or other business listings, you might want to structure a name that will appear high in the list.

- Is it a cliché? Try to avoid overused word roots such as pro, ultra, tech, global, and the like.

- Does it limit you? You probably don't know exactly what direction your business may take. If you create a name that is too specific, it may make it harder to keep your identity as you expand or move into other business activities. For example, "The Soccer Shop" may be limiting if that business decides to sell other sports equipment.

- Is it tied to a trend? If you tie your name to a trend, you're stuck when the trend changes. For example, in the mid-1980s and early 1990s, many high-tech companies wanted to communicate that they were on top of cutting edge technology, so they added "2000" to their name, associating with the coming millennium. The problem is that at least one of these companies, Gateway 2000, became quite large and continued doing business after the turn of the millennium. So Gateway 2000 changed its name to simply "Gateway."

Your business name doesn't have to meet all these criteria, but these questions at least give you a way to start thinking about it.

Resources

NameRazor
http://www.NameRazor.com
This software helps you pick a name for your business, website, Internet domain, or even your boat. It uses a database of nearly 1,000 "namelets" and allows you to use an unlimited number of keywords as it works to generate names.

2. Create a logo

At some point in the life of your business, you may decide to take your brand building to the next level by creating a logo. A logo is visual reinforcement of your business image. In a visually oriented society, logos provide one more way for potential customers to remember your business.

A logo furnishes another valuable service. It provides a symbol around which you can rally your confidence, focus your creativity, and reinforce your vision for your business. In addition to catching your customer's interest, the logo you create should inspire you, your partners, your employees, and even your vendors.

You don't have to have a logo the first day you start your business. You may want to build your business for a while and see what direction it takes you before committing to a specific design. When you're ready, designing a logo does not have to cost a fortune. You could do it yourself. However, unless you are a graphic artist or designer by trade, it's probably a better idea to hire a professional designer. Even if you are a graphic artist or designer, you might want to get some fresh, outside design ideas.

Many low-cost logo design companies are available through the Internet. You can also engage a design or art school to determine whether designing your company logo could be a project for one of their classes. This design project would provide you with a free or low-cost logo while giving new designers the chance to build their portfolios.

Regardless of how you do it, here are some very basic principles for designing a logo:

- Make sure it's dissimilar. Avoid costly litigation by ensuring your logo does not resemble that of another company or organization.

- Create a color and a black-and-white version. Add a splash to your business cards and correspondence by including color in your logo. In addition, have a black-and-white version that will look good in a fax or other situations in which color reproduction is not available.

- Make it scalable. People should be able to distinguish your logo regardless of its size.

Resources

LogoWorks

http://www.LogoWorks.com
LogoWorks will design a logo for your company for $295 to $495. The company also designs stationary, websites, and brochures.

Sticky Concepts

http://www.stickyconcepts.com

For $249, Sticky Concepts provides four full-color logo concepts, four adjustment cycles, one redraw, and a private page located within its site to view your concepts.

3. Show your face

Another part of your branding is your face. By including your picture on communication media such as your website, brochure, and business card, you make it easier for potential clients to identify you in public. Someone may briefly come in contact with your photograph on your website or in a brochure and, sometime later, remember your face at your child's soccer game or a professional meeting. By displaying your photograph with your business materials, you give potential customers a chance to associate not only your business name and your logo but also your face with your services and products.

Real estate agents are particularly adept at putting their photographs on their business cards and other materials. Thus clients can identify them at community functions or when they are meeting them at a house for the first time. For a more whimsical spin, you can have an artist make a line drawing or cartoon of your likeness. Artists do this kind of thing at carnivals and other family events, but you can also commission an artist for your business, perhaps including some prop that represents what you do.

In Practice

When Joe Barranco started a new real estate business in the Chicago area, he was looking for an identity that would stand out from the crowd. That's when he became the "Rockin' Realtor." As Joe describes it, "Most realtors use a tag line to describe their business. I wanted to use something memorable that the public could relate to." So Joe combined his hobby playing rock guitar with his new business to brand himself as the Rockin' Realtor.

To announce his business, Joe decided to create a realty newsletter for his customers and prospects, but he needed a picture to go with his new tag line. While going through some old things, he found a caricature of himself playing guitar. It was drawn by a cartoonist sometime in 1976. "To tell the truth, I'm not exactly sure where I got the drawing. It might have been at the auto show that year." Regardless of its pedigree, the drawing was the kind of light-hearted image Joe was looking for.

He took the drawing to a print shop specializing in real estate marketing materials, where it was scanned and added to his newsletter layout. Since then, he's published several issues of the newsletter. He estimates he spends about 12 hours preparing the content and pays the print shop about $180 per issue to set up the layout. His mailing list comprises names he drew from organizations, personal contacts, his church directory, and purchased lists.

Although it represents a fairly significant time investment every month, Joe figures the Rockin' Realtor has paid off. "Everyone I know who has received a copy said they liked it and I can trace four new clients who said they liked the Rockin' Realtor concept so much, it influenced their decision to do business with me," Joe says. To help defray the costs, Joe sells advertising in his newsletter. "I think if I get two more sponsors, the newsletter will pay for itself." Rock on Joe!

4. Redefine your title

Don't assume that because you are trained in one field and you've found a particular niche, that your business may not apply to a completely different industry or niche. The only difference may be in your title or the way you describe your skills on your resume. For example, here's an advertisement for a business analyst consulting project:

> "Seeking a business analyst consultant with eCommerce experience to translate business objectives into clear and concise documentation and structured models. Works closely with assigned project manager and team leads to translate and document business requirements into detailed functional requirements."

Although the project is for a "business analyst," the skills described could easily fit those for a technical writer ("document business requirements…") or a business marketing writer ("translate business objectives…").

In the article "Brave New Job Hunt" in the September 23, 2002, *Newsweek* (p. 55), Bernadette Kenny, executive vice president at Lee Hecht Harrison, an outplacement firm, stated "The skills may be transferable, but the words on the resume may not be." According to the article, Kenny's team "teaches job applicants to describe their skills in terms that other industries can understand." If you focus on your real skills or different ways you can apply your products or services for a new group of customers, you can open up whole new markets for your business.

Analyze your skills, product descriptions, and services to discover other industries or niches to which they may apply. Then, start reading publications, visiting websites, and checking Internet discussion boards in those industries for any opportunities to introduce yourself and what you do.

5. Incorporate your business

In addition to the liability and tax advantages to incorporating, this legal form of business helps reinforce your brand. There's something about having Inc., Incorporated, Corp. or Corporation after your business name that carries a certain cachet. It communicates stability, credibility, and your commitment to the success of your business. When you incorporate, clients, vendors, and other businesses may perceive your business as much larger and more credible.

Resources

The Company Corporation
http://www.incorporate.com
In addition to 25 offices across the country, The Company Corporation and its affiliated companies provide an online form with which you can incorporate in any state for as little as $199. The company also conducts trademark searches and has a strategic alliance with the Service Corps of Retired Executives (SCORE).

Nolo Press
http://www.nolo.com
Besides publishing many books on incorporating, this website has a wealth of articles and resources on the legal aspects of running a business.

6.   Become a reseller

You can expand your product and service offerings by becoming a Value Added Reseller (VAR). As a VAR, you might provide a variety of services that include selling, configuring, installing, and maintaining a product. If you can meet the producing vendor's requirements, as a VAR the product you sell can carry some prestige. You might also benefit from the producing vendor's advertising budget.

However, keep in mind that, depending on the type of product, you may be committing to added responsibilities. For example, if you decide to become a VAR for a technology product, you may be required to be on call around the clock. You may have to provide training for the product and you may have to hire more employees so you can provide customer service while you are on vacation or working with other clients.

Resources

Association for Linux Value Added Resellers

http://www.linuxvar.org

The Information Technology (IT) industry has many VAR programs built around hardware and software products. The Linux VAR association supports those who provide VAR solutions to customers using the Linux operating system. They act as a referral service, matching customers with the appropriate VAR or multiple VARs who offer Linux-based solutions.

7. Offer a service agreement

If you sell a product or service that requires ongoing maintenance, you could offer a service agreement. There are many structures for this type of agreement, but in the most common form of service agreement the client pays in advance for a predefined number of your hours at a discounted rate. The advantage of this type of agreement for clients is that they are guaranteed a set amount of your time and they get a predetermined, discounted rate. The advantage for you is a steadier cash flow for your business.

A different spin on the service agreement is a retainer. Under a retainer agreement, you regularly bill the client a fixed fee in exchange for being available to the client on an as-needed basis. However, typically the client is not allowed to carry over unused time. This is common in the legal, public relations, and advertising fields. As with the service agreement, the main advantage for you is a consistent cash flow.

Here are some ways you can offer a service agreement:

- **Package deals.** Offer varying packages of hours, each with ascending discount rates. The more hours a client pre-pays, the cheaper the rate.

- **Customer service phone.** Add a toll-free service number to your business, then charge a fixed monthly fee for a client to use the number to call you for help. Rather than sit by the phone, you can forward calls to your mobile phone or to another location where you're working. Be sure to identify the hours that you will be available to help those who call.

- **Regular maintenance.** Identify repetitive maintenance tasks that the client may not want to do and bill these tasks on a fixed monthly schedule. For example, a programmer can include regular backups of the client's data. A dog walker can offer a fur- and nail-trimming service.

If you decide to offer a service or retainer agreement, there are several things to consider:

1. What discount on your hours will you give?

2. Will you allow clients to maintain a balance and "carry over" unused hours or will they expire after a period of time?

3. Will you offer the service agreement for any task or only for specific tasks?

8. Start a new product through licensing

Want to jump-start your business? Consider licensing the rights to a product or technology developed by someone else. This saves you time and money in research and development costs and helps you bring a new product to market in less time. Many universities and other companies provide technology-transfer opportunities, and there are Internet marketplaces that play matchmaker between licensing entities and entrepreneurs looking for new products.

Do your due diligence. Before you consider licensing a new technology, ask these questions:

- **Does it work?** Don't accept the claims of the technology owner without performing your own tests or hiring someone to put the product or technology through its paces.
- **Who will buy it?** Determine whether there is a market for a product made from the new technology. Does anyone else have a similar technology? Can you grow the market?
- **Can you make it profitable?** The technology may be great, but if you find out it will cost a great deal more than anyone is willing to pay to produce it, it's not practical to bring the product to market.
- **Are there any regulatory issues?** If the product requires lengthy government approval, you have to factor the time and cost of getting this approval into your business plan.

Resources

Uventures.com

http://www.Uventures.com
This site connects those seeking cutting-edge technologies with the universities and institutions that are developing these innovations. Through its website, Uventures creates an accessible market for new technologies and provides a source of information for the technology transfer industry.

QX

http://www.Qxhealth.com
This site, owned by Uventures.com, focuses on licensing for the pharmaceutical and healthcare industries.

9. Trademark your product or service

As you do business and accumulate customers, you are building your special brand. To protect your brand from other businesses that inadvertently or purposely hitchhike on the success of your business, you can trademark your product or service.

To engage in the trademark process, you can conduct a trademark search yourself and submit your own trademark application to the U.S. Department of Commerce Patent and Trademark Office. However, you may want to use a skilled attorney as your consultant or representative.

In Practice

What's in a name? Perhaps an opportunity to change client perceptions. That's the strategy adopted by Tom Anderson, co-owner of Real Work Business Results, Inc. As consultants in business process redesign and management training, Anderson and his partner were looking for a way to communicate their value-based approach to consulting. So they trademarked two phrases that they use in their branding: "...a Resulting (not consulting) company" and "Resultant (not consultant)."

Anderson and his partner developed these phrases after reflecting on their own experience in hiring consultants. "We call ourselves Resultants (not consultants) for a reason. Both of us used to be line managers, and we've both suffered through our fair share of 'consulting interventions.' We've listened to what our clients want from a resulting company and watched what the consulting industry standard for 'client service' has become."

Anderson believes their trademarked phrases help them avoid the negative stigma some consultants have earned, while at the same time opening some doors for their business. "Our brand leverages the bad reputation of many consultants and gets us invitations to speak and introductions to decision makers."

Resources

Sci3

http://www.sci3.com
For a fee, Sci3 provides custom patent and trademark search services. The operation is part of the Sunnyvale Center for Innovation, Invention, and Ideas (SCI3). The center is located in the Sunnyvale, California, Public Library which has a relationship with the United States Patent and Trademark Office as a Patent and Trademark Library. If you plan to be in the Silicon Valley area, sign up for any of Sci3's seminars on patents and trademarks.

United States Patent & Trademark Office

http://www.uspto.gov

From this site, you can search patents, expired patents, trademarks, and USPC Classification codes to get a definition of a patent class. The site also provides forms to download and a registry of patent attorneys and agents.

Nolo Press

http://www.nolo.com

The Nolo Press publishes books about contracts and the law for non-lawyers. In addition, the website includes software, forms, dictionaries, and articles on everyday legal topics.

Trademark: Legal Care for Your Business & Product Name

by Stephen R. Elias. Berkeley, CA: Nolo Press, 5th ed., 2001.
ISBN 0-87337-579-3.

This comprehensive Nolo handbook provides the most up-to-date information on defending your intellectual property. This updated version includes a chapter on how the Internet is affecting both trademark law and decisions on choosing a trademark. The book also provides step-by-step instructions for using the Patent and Trademark Office's free Internet database to perform trademark searches, and information on the PTO's new online trademark application filing utility, eTEAS. The book includes all necessary forms and instructions to register a trademark or service mark with the U.S. Patent & Trademark Office.

10. Franchise

Franchising is no longer for fast-food restaurants only. All kinds of businesses are going the franchise route. With franchising you can expand your business more quickly with less financial risk than with traditional means. With franchising the costs of expanding a business into new markets are lower because the startup costs of any new extension are shared with the franchisee. Often, the franchisor and the franchisee can combine their purchasing power to negotiate lower costs with suppliers.

How do you know whether your business is appropriate for franchising? Here are some questions to ask yourself:

• Do you have a proven business concept that can be applied more than once?

- Can your business be duplicated and easily taught?
- Does your business have a unique niche?
- Is there room for growth in your market?
- Does your business have "curb appeal"; i.e., is it a business in which a potential franchisee will see profit potential and pride in ownership.
- Is your business capable of supporting the franchisee with a fair return on investment and a decent living?

If you answered "yes" to most of these questions, franchising may be worth considering. Be prepared though. If you take this route, running the franchising business may well become your core business.

Resources

Entrepreneur.com

http://www.entrepreneur.com
From the publishers of *Entrepreneur* magazine, this website features a wealth of franchising and other small-business information.

The Entrepreneur's Source

http://www.franchiseexperts.com
This website is itself a franchise, created to help match franchisers with franchisees. The site provides services to package, launch, and maintain a successful and profitable franchise business. These services include feasibility assessment, business planning, raising capital, regulatory compliance, marketing and advertising, lead generation, candidate qualification, and expansion plans.

Franchising & Licensing: Two Ways to Build Your Business

by Andrew J. Sherman. AMACOM, 2nd ed., 1999. ISBN 0814404502. This book provides a strategic guide for developing a business growth plan and making the most of intellectual property through franchising and licensing. Subjects include protection of intellectual property, field support, regulatory compliance, co-branding strategies, quality control systems, mergers and acquisitions, international expansion, and litigation.

Franchising for Dummies

by Michael Seid and Dave Thomas. New York: John Wiley & Sons, 2000, ISBN 0764551604.

Written in the Dummies style, this book features two industry experts. Michael Seid, a well-known consultant with 20 years in the field, and Dave Thomas, the founder of Wendy's, provide inside tips from their personal experience.

Maintaining a High Profile

"An identity would seem to be arrived at by the way in which the person faces and uses his experience."
—James Baldwin (1924–87), U.S. author. *The Price of the Ticket*, "No Name in the Street" (1985; first published 1972).

The best way to advertise your business is to maintain a high profile. To do this, hone your writing and presentation skills and reinforce your expert status by writing articles and giving seminars. While the publicity value of writing an article or giving a seminar can often justify the effort, with a little extra packaging you can turn your intellectual property into another revenue stream.

11. Write articles

If you believe your written communication skills are good, propose to write articles for an industry publication. Such articles help your business in two major ways. First, writing articles in a publication likely to be read by your customer base is the best way to establish yourself as an expert in your field. Second, most major publications pay their writers for their articles, so this becomes another revenue stream.

To prepare an article proposal, obtain a previous edition of the publication and thoroughly read it, paying attention to not only the articles but also the kind of advertising run. Find the copyright page, which usually lists the editorial staff and note the name of the editors. This page may even provide Writer Guidelines. The Writer Guidelines will explain the proper procedure for submitting an article idea to the publication. If they have one, call or write to them and request a copy. Then, propose your article by writing a query letter to the editor. This is where you pitch your article idea and describe your qualifications to write the article.

What should you write about? You could propose a case study of how you solved a customer problem that may apply to others in the same industry. You could write a review of a new software product or book applicable to the publication's readership. You could prepare a profile of an important industry leader. Use your imagination, and you'll be surprised how many ideas you'll come up with.

Resources

Writers Market Website

http://www.writersmarket.com

This site provides search capabilities for publishing outlets listed in the Writer's Market series of books including markets that are not in the print version. When you purchase the book, you automatically receive a one-year subscription to the website, or you can purchase a subscription separately on the site.

Writer's Market

by Katie Struckel Brogan (Editor), Robert Brewer. Writers Digest Books, ISBN: 158297120X.

Published yearly, this guide includes more than 1,534 consumer magazines and 464 trade magazines. It includes articles about query letters, book proposals, and freelance article rates.

How to Write Irresistible Query Letters

by Lisa Collier Cool. F&W Publications, January 2002, ISBN 1582971552. Written by a successful author and literary agent, this book provides practical advice on how to write query letters that sell your article ideas.

12. Offer seminars and training

Even if training is not one of your core services, someone will pay you for your knowledge if it will solve a problem or save them time and/or money. This not only provides another source of revenue for your business, but also helps to market your core business. You can train people either in small groups, in one-on-one sessions, or in a classroom. The least expensive approaches are small informal groups or one-on-one sessions. In these situations, you can tailor the training to the needs of your student or students. If you decide to do classroom training, you can either develop an entire program yourself or be hired as an instructor for a pre-designed course offered by an institution or professional training company.

There's a distinction between providing a seminar and teaching a class. Seminars are typically short, from 1 hour to 2 weeks, and feature a tightly focused subject. On the other hand, a class deals with a more general subject taught over a longer period of time. Many for-credit institutions require credentialed instructors to teach their classes. To avoid this problem, you could teach a noncredit course to students in the institution's continuing education program or approach a community college that encourages professionals outside the education field to teach at their institutions. Some of these institutions seek instructors to teach courses already in their program, while others are open to new course proposals. If you decide to propose a course, keep in mind that these institutions schedule their programs far in advance. Also, check the institution's policy on promoting your business in the classroom.

The advantage of creating your own seminar or class is that you control the material and collect all the money. Also, you can use the seminar to promote your consulting business. However, be prepared to do a lot of work and spend some money to set up the seminar. In developing the course content, you have to create and print course materials, rent classroom space, and handle registration.

The advantage of teaching a pre-designed course through contracting with a local institution or a professional training company is that you do not have to create the content and manage the registration. However, when you contract with an institution or training company, you make less money than you would with your own program and the institution or training company may impose restrictions on your marketing activities. Also, to teach a course for a professional training company, you might have to be certified in the particular product.

What should you teach? One option is to offer seminars or training in the tools and techniques that you regularly use. For example, if you're a programmer, you use a particular development tool to write code. You could train other programmers to use the tool and show them programming techniques. If you're a painter, you can train someone to do faux painting. How often have you been at a party or other social event and someone asked you how to start a business similar to yours? If you are not worried about creating competition, another option is to train someone to set up a business similar to yours. While this one-on-one training is not quite like franchising (because you don't continue to collect royalties after you set up the business), you can still make money by training people who want to avoid the mistakes you made.

The following are some potential sources for training:

- Your software shelves, your toolbox, or tool shed. Are you confident about your skills with a particular software program? Is there a particular tool or set of tools that are tricky to use such that someone might pay you to show him or her how to use it? Do you have a special technique that you could teach to someone?

- Local community college. Look up local community colleges in your phone book. Get a catalog of their courses and determine whether they offer courses in something at which you are an expert. If they don't, determine whether it's worth proposing a new course. Find out whom to contact at the school about your proposal.

- Local stores. Any stores that sell parts, equipment, and materials for do-it-yourself jobs are good candidates for a training class proposal. Types of stores include garden centers, building supply stores, hardware stores, hobby stores, and music shops. If you are a landscaper, contact the local garden center to determine whether they will sponsor gardening classes. If you are a carpenter, contact the local building supply chain to determine whether you can offer carpentry classes through the store.

- Software vendors. Software companies such as Microsoft, Adobe, Cisco, and Macromedia offer training certificate programs, either directly or through approved training facilities, for teaching classes on various software products. With this credential, you can approach professional training companies to do part-time training in these products.

13. Conduct a telephone seminar

With the costs of on-site seminars rising, a viable alternative is a telephone seminar. In a telephone seminar, participants call into a conference center at a specified time, and the speaker makes the presentation from the convenience of his or her home office. The obvious disadvantage of a telephone seminar is that it is audio only. You cannot project slides, use a wipe board, or watch for nonverbal feedback from the audience. The presentation is similar to that of a radio broadcast. However, most telephone seminar service providers allow two-way communication in a question-and-answer segment. Despite the fact that you cannot project slides in a telephone seminar, you can distribute materials to the participants prior to the presentation and refer to specific pages, slides, and graphics during the presentation.

Unless you have the equipment and the telephone lines to conduct this kind of seminar yourself, you should use a conference service provider. These service providers usually charge a flat monthly fee or per-person for single events. Because there is a cost involved, you have to decide whether you want to charge for the seminar or offer it free as a form of advertising for your business.

Resources

KRM Information Services

http://www.krm.com

This company provides the technical resources for conducting audio and audio-plus-Web seminars. It also assists in promoting your event through blast e-mail and blast fax services. For follow-up sales, the company produces audio tapes, CD-ROMs, or Web-based archives of your presentation for those who were unable to attend or as future reference for those who did attend.

14. Publish a book through a publisher

If you are a good writer, are willing to put in the time, and have a lot of patience, you can write a book about your field and perhaps interest a publisher. If you decide to tackle a book, be realistic. Writing a book is more time consuming and psychologically draining than any other type of writing.

By consulting *The Writers Market,* you can find out which publishers are appropriate for your book proposal and their procedures for contacting them. Because publishers receive so many book proposals, you may want to enlist the services of an agent. A good agent can use his or her contacts to help you get your foot in the door. However, you have to sell a good agent on the idea of representing your book just as much as you would have to sell a publisher on printing it. Even if a publisher shows interest in your book, be prepared to wait a long time for an answer. Publishers can take several months or longer to decide whether to publish your manuscript.

Resources

Agents, Editors and You: The Insider's Guide to Getting Your Book Published

by Michelle Howry (Editor). Writers Digest Books, 2002, ISBN 1582971528.

Published by the same company that publishes The Writers Market every year, this book helps you line up an agent. The book includes interviews with successful agents and editors. It provides information about submitting, selling, and publishing your manuscript, and contemporary trends in publishing such as e-queries, e-publishing, and self-publishing.

15. Self-publish a book

Benjamin Franklin, Walt Whitman, D.H. Lawrence, and Mark Twain all did it, so why not you? All these famous writers self-published at least one of their books. If you can't interest a publisher or agent in your manuscript and you're willing to invest additional time and money into the project, consider self-publishing your book.

Be prepared. When you go down the path of self-publishing, you are not only expressing yourself through the art of writing, but also creating an entirely new business. Self-publishing can add some additional revenue to your core business, but it has its own demands. As with your core business, you have to take time and money to market your book. Considering that every year more than 70,000 books are published and you are competing with television, movies, the Internet, and video games for people's attention, this is no easy feat. In addition, you have to manage the production, storage, and fulfillment (filling orders) of a physical product.

However, there are several advantages to self-publishing:

• **Shorter publishing cycle.** Because it takes larger publishing companies a long time to decide whether to publish your book and at least six months to actually get it into print, you can save a lot of time by self-publishing and avoiding the "committee review" period.

- **Rights.** If you contract with a publisher, you will transfer your copyrights to the publisher in exchange for royalty payments. If you self-publish, you retain all your rights, which you can negotiate to sell at any time for your own benefit.

- **Creative control.** When you work with a publisher, the publisher's editors and designers have much control over the layout, cover design, and writing tone of the final product. If you self-publish, you decide on the look and feel of the final product.

- **Money. Most publishers offer a 5%–15% royalty payment.** What do they offer for that concession? Granted, they finance the production and distribution of the book, but believe it or not, most publishers put very little money or effort into marketing new, unknown authors. So, even with a publisher, you will spend much of your own time marketing the book. If you self-publish, after accounting for cost of production, distribution, and marketing, you can make 20%–80% on books you sell.

- **Avenue to a larger publisher.** Many larger publishers are more interested in publishing a book that is already in print than in publishing a raw manuscript, because it is a finished product that may have already established an audience. Some very successful authors have launched their writing careers by first self-publishing and then selling their book rights to a larger publisher that is willing to put more effort into the marketing and distribution of the book.

In addition to regular print publishing, there is the whole new world of e-publishing and Print on Demand (POD). E-publishing is the creation of a book in a purely electronic medium. This can be a book on CD or one downloaded from the Internet. There are many competing formats that seek to maintain the book owner's rights by thwarting copying, but the advantage of e-publishing is there are virtually no production costs. POD publication uses a xerographic printing method to produce paper books from electronic files. The cost of equipment to accomplish this is out of the reach of most individual self-publishers. However, using this technology through a POD printer, you can produce books one at a time as they are ordered or print very small batches of books. Although the cost to produce each book is higher, the main advantage of POD production is that you don't have to pay for and store a garage full of books before you can sell them.

Resources

Complete Guide to Self Publishing: Everything You Need to Know to Write, Publish, Promote, and Sell Your Own Book

by Tom and Marilyn Ross. Buena Vista, CO: F&W Publications, 4th rev. ed., 2002, ISBN 1582970912.

In their fourth edition of this well-sold book, the Rosses provide a blueprint for publishing your own book.

The Self-Publishing Manual: How to Write, Print and Sell Your Own Book (13th Ed)

by Dan Poynter. Para Publishing, 13th ed., 2001, ISBN 1568600739.

A well-established and well-known authority on self-publishing, Dan Poynter, has written about this subject for years. In his 13th edition of this classic how-to book, he covers contemporary subjects like "multipurposing" your book into CD and e-book formats.

Make Money Self-Publishing : Learn How from Fourteen Successful Small Publishers

by Suzanne P. Thomas. Boulder, CO: Gemstone House Publishing, 2001, ISBN 0966469127.

This book profiles, in explicit detail, 14 successful small publishing ventures that started from scratch. It answers all the questions that other books don't. Want to know how the publisher got an idea for a book? Want to know how many copies were printed in the first run? Which distributors worked and which didn't? Want to know how the publishers decided when to hire additional help? This book answers all these and many more questions. All the profiled publishers are average people. Most of them did not have any previous publishing experience and many had never written a book before.

Poor Richard's Creating E-Books

by Chris Van Buren and Jeff Cogswell. Lakewood, CO: Top Floor Publishing, 2001, ISBN 1930082029.

Written in an easy-to-read tone, this book provides an excellent overview of the e-book and Print on Demand (POD) marketplace.

1001 Ways to Market Your Books

by John Kremer. Lakewood, CO: Open Horizons, 5th ed, 2001, ISBN 0912411481.

Because marketing your book is key to its success, make sure you read this book before you embark on your publishing venture. This book provides tons of ideas for marketing to bookstores, libraries, gift outlets, and online.

Amazon Advantage program

http://www.amazon.com/exec/obidos/subst/partners/direct /advantage-for-books.html.

The Amazon.com Advantage program provides a great marketplace for your books. In exchange for a 55% discount rate off list price, Amazon lists your book on its website and maintains a small inventory in the warehouses so buyers can take advantage of 24-hour shipping turnaround. If you think the discount rate is too high, you can sell your books on Amazon through a distributor such as Ingram or Baker and Taylor.

16. Produce Your Own Audio Product

As in publishing your own book, you can produce your own audio cassette or audio CD. The advantage of audio production is that it is relatively inexpensive to create a product for distribution. You can make your production simple or elaborate. You can use a quiet room to record your audio production on a simple cassette recorder, or you can rent space in a recording studio.

Recording on an analog cassette tape is not the only option. Cheap computer technology combined with inexpensive CD recording equipment and new digital recording formats allow you to create digital audio. You can record directly onto your computer and save the file in MP3, WAV, or similar digital format. Then you can either sell your recording on your website, where paying customers can directly download it, or record it directly onto a CD-R and mail it to ordering customers.

What should you record? Your audio production can use several models, as follows:

• **The interview.** You can have someone interview you about key issues relevant to your industry.

- **The seminar.** Record a seminar that you're going to present. This leverages the material you created for the seminar and helps you present the seminar's message to a larger audience.

- **The audio magazine.** Record a broadcast with industry stories including interviews with industry leaders, how-to sessions, and industry news. If you can maintain the pace, you can release these recordings on a monthly or quarterly schedule.

- **The how-to manual.** Describe how to accomplish a specific set of tasks. The subject you choose must be translatable to the audio format, but you can supplement the audio with a paper training guide that may include pictures.

Resources

Words on Tape: How to Create Profitable Spoken Word Audio on Cassettes and CDs
by Judy Byers. Audio Cassette Producers; 1 edition, 1997. ISBN: 0965572145

This book provides a basic road map to create an audio product. It covers creating the script, recording, editing, mastering the tapes, duplication, and packaging.

Producing and Selling Your Own Audio Cassette (Single Tape Speaking Series)
by Gordon Burgett. Communication Unlimited, 2nd ed., 1996, ISBN 0910167125.

This audio cassette steps you through the production of an audio cassette, including production and sales. It also covers royalties, copyright, piracy, dub masters, and much more.

17. Spell-check and proof everything!

Maintaining a high profile through your writing means putting extra effort into the quality of your text. Although most people understand the need to spell check and proof read important business communications such as brochures or mass-mail printed letters, e-mail is the correspondence most vulnerable to typos. In the hurry of wanting to send a message to someone or respond to an e-mail query, it's easy to get sloppy and put speed of response over quality of writing.

Most businesses exist to solve client or customer problems. This is especially true for consultants. Next to conversation, your written correspondence is the primary means of communication with your clients, customers, and prospects. Therefore, people will judge you and your business on your ability to communicate. If you take the time to spell-check and proofread even your quick e-mail responses, you communicate to your correspondents that you care about quality and are thorough about your work.

Don't rely only on your spell checker! Spell checkers can be wrong. Most spell checkers offer the ability to add words to their dictionary. This is useful to keep your spell checker from flagging special industry jargon not common in standard dictionaries. However, if you are not careful with this feature, you can actually introduce a misspelled word that the spell checker will assume is correct! Even if you have an excellent spell checker, it will not flag a situation where you typed the wrong word if the word you typed is spelled correctly. For example, if you wanted to type

"We think the problem occurred in the venting system."

but instead you typed

"We thing the problem occurred in the venting system."

Your spell checker will not flag the word "thing." Some word processors include a grammar checker that might catch the above mistake, but no electronic method can reliably substitute for a human proofreader.

Make sure you spell check your e-mail correspondence and re-read your messages before you click the send button. In addition, check every page of your website and any auto responders you have in place for typos. If possible, have someone other than the author check these materials before you release them to the public. When you proof your own work, it is easier to gloss over some typos.

Marketing Through Pricing

"The cost of a thing is the amount of what I will call life which is required to be exchanged for it, immediately or in the long run."
—Henry David Thoreau (1817–62), U.S. philosopher, author, naturalist. *Walden*, "Economy" (1854).

How you price your products and/or services is a form of marketing in itself. However, in most cases, your pricing strategy must include more than simply offering the lowest price. In some, primarily commodity-based, businesses, price is a major issue. On the other hand, in some consulting businesses, experienced practitioners believe that clients don't take low-priced consultants seriously. Million-dollar consultants rely on value-based pricing to break through the "hourly-rate ceiling." Keep in mind that many studies show that people rarely make purchase decisions on price alone, so you typically cannot base your entire business strategy on price.

There are many different ways you can use pricing to increase market share and/or profits. To increase market share and extend your marketing, become a wholesaler and discount your price for distributors. This practice is common for manufacturers that have access to a distribution channel, but it can also be applied to services. For example, in the case of consultants, wholesaling is done through agencies or job brokers. Another way you can market through pricing is in the way you get paid. You can provide a more flexible arrangement for a client by bidding a project on a fixed bid rather than on an hourly basis.

As the economy goes through its inevitable ups and down, you also will have to remain flexible in your pricing. Deciding to cut your price, whether as a standard discount, an incentive, or for survival, is something you will have to face at some point in the life of your business. However, you can creatively cut your price and still realize a fair profit.

18. Base your pricing on value

Basing your fees or compensation on commodity measurements such as hours, days, projects, personnel, and the like creates an artificial ceiling to your revenue. After all, there are only so many hours in the day, days in the week. Expert consultants who reach the seven-figure incomes usually do so by abandoning objective measures such as dollars per hour and adopting a business model that uses value-based pricing.

To make this method work, you have to change some old habits. Because you won't know what to charge until you establish how the client will value your work, you must have the discipline not to quote clients a price, even a "ballpark" price, right away. You must identify quantitative amounts or qualitative effects for a successful client outcome as defined by the client.

Most successful, value-based pricing is based on good, old-fashioned ROI. There are two basic ways to get ROI: save the client money by reducing costs and/or increase the client's revenues. Once you quantify the ROI, you can negotiate a profitable rate based on this value. Another key factor of successful value-based pricing is the ability to measure the results. Make sure you can measure results based on savings, incremental sales, or gross percentage of sales.

Resources

Value-Based Fees: How to Charge—and Get—What You're Worth
by Alan Weiss. Jossey-Bass, January 2002, ISBN 0787955116.
Part of the Ultimate Consultant series, this book, written by million dollar consultant Alan Weiss, shows you how to move beyond the old "time plus materials" concept of consulting compensation to a model that establishes fees based on value delivered to improve the client's condition.

In Practice

In an environment in which clients are hesitant to take a chance on a small company and the competition is fierce, Chris Young struck upon a business model that has increased profits for both him and his clients. As he explains it, "We put our money where our mouth is by basing our compensation on a piece of the ROI."

Young is founder of The Rainmaker Group, a Bismarck, North Dakota, people development organization that provides training in customer service, team building, and sales training. When he was looking for a way to connect with larger clients, Young ended up creating a whole new business model for his company. "We met with a company in the weight-loss business. After reviewing the call center operation, we were confident that we could increase their revenue by changing the way they responded to their clients. However, we were relatively new in business and didn't have a lot of client case studies to back up our story," he says.

So what did Young do to get the business? He got creative. "We proposed taking a small stipend up front and basing the rest of our compensation on a percentage of the ROI." The client loved the idea. Rather than looking like consultants trying to take the client's money, they became, in effect, the client's partners. As Young points out, "It was a win-win scenario. The client pays a little on the front end and then pays for performance on the back end." And it certainly paid off for Chris and his company. "We earned approximately $50,000 for a 4-month project," he says.

Since then, Young has applied his ROI value-based business model to other clients. "We're currently working with a company in the chiropractic industry. We saw a way to expand an underutilized service they offer by training a new sales representative. We based the majority of our compensation on the additional sales we generated." This strategy also makes his company very competitive. "In the training and development consulting world, I believe this is innovative. Nobody else will do what we do."

For the ROI model to work, Young has to identify clients for whom he's sure he can increase revenue and can measure the results based on either incremental sales or gross percentage of sales. "The percentage of ROI we negotiate varies based on time and resources needed to implement the plan. We shoot for a result equal to three or four times our hourly bill rate," he says.

Although he's moving towards a "straight ROI" model where he does not charge an up-front stipend, Young is sticking with the current model for now. "Moving to strait ROI makes me nervous. Right now, the model works with a combination of stipend plus ROI, but we're adjusting our model to eventually move to straight ROI."

19. Offer a guarantee

To stand behind your work, offer a guarantee. It can be a money-back guarantee for a physical product or an agreement to re-do some work if it's a service. Guarantees are particularly useful if your prospects are not familiar with you or your product; then you need to offer an additional incentive for them to "take a chance on you." Some business owners may be instinctually hesitant to offer unrestricted guarantees for fear of abuse, but experience has shown that most clients and customers do not abuse fair guarantees.

When you offer a guarantee, you need to consider the following:

- Will the guarantee be "no questions asked," or will you require a reason? You might want to request an explanation, not as a barrier to offering the guarantee, but as a form of market research, so you can improve your product or service.
- Will there be a time limit for the guarantee or will it be a "lifetime" guarantee?
- Are there extensive costs or liability issues involved with the exercise of the guarantee? If the product or service is simple and innocuous, you can request that the customer send the product back or re-do the service. However, if the product is complicated and the customer's wear-and-tear on the product has to be taken into consideration, you may want to include restrictions. Consult an attorney to write the appropriate guarantee provisions.

The following are some suggestions for offering a guarantee:

- **Carrot and stick.** The client may stipulate a cash penalty for late delivery. If so, try to also stipulate a reciprocating cash bonus for early completion.
- **Insurance.** If they are feasible, a performance bond or errors and omissions insurance can be used to cover your work. Performance bonds and errors and omissions insurance are purchased from insurance companies, but these policies are expensive. If the insurance is necessary only for a particular client, you can try to negotiate to have the client pay for part or all of the cost.

- **Property rights.** If you are selling a product or service of significant value and you offer a money-back guarantee, you should require that the customer return the product before the refund is issued or specify that all property rights to any deliverable you've provided revert to you.
- **Stepped guarantee.** For a project-based service, you can break the project into stages at which the money-back guarantee expires after the client accepts completion of each step. You can signify acceptance by requiring the client to "sign off" at the completion of each stage.

20. Provide a nonprofit discount

In addition to volunteering and doing pro bono work, you can offer a discount to nonprofit organizations. Perhaps your service or product is directly useful to a nonprofit and the organization becomes your target customer. For example, if you are a programmer who has developed a database program that helps nonprofits track their donors, you're going to primarily market to non-profits anyway.

You can volunteer to do free work for your favorite nonprofits or give away free product to the right charity, but you certainly can't spread yourself too thin by giving away all your services and/or products. Don't assume that because it's a nonprofit, the organization doesn't have a budget to pay something for your services. You can make it more affordable for nonprofits to do business with you while helping your community by offering a special discount to nonprofits. Doing this adds to your customer list and portfolio of work.

21. Sell wholesale through agencies

You can extend your reach and open new markets by selling your services wholesale. Wholesaling is a common practice for manufacturers that have access to a distribution channel, but it can also be applied to services. If you're a consultant, the wholesale rate is the rate you charge the agencies that subcontract work to you. An agency is a company that places contract employees on assignments with its clients. Agencies are also called consulting firms, job shops, and brokers. Whatever the name, they typically will play a part in your marketing plan, particularly in the early years of your business.

From a marketing standpoint, free agents act as wholesalers to agencies. You should establish one rate for your direct clients and another, lower rate for agencies. Agencies generally mark up your rate from 20% to 100% in the same way a distributor or retailer marks up the wholesale price of a product.

There are several advantages to using agencies:

- **You can often find work quickly.** Particularly in the early years of your consulting business, agencies can provide work quickly while you establish yourself.

- **They buffer you from the client.** Most agencies must carry proper business liability and workers compensation insurance. Some even carry professional liability (i.e., errors and omissions) insurance to cover worker's mistakes. This insurance buffers you somewhat from client litigation. Finally, if there is a personality conflict between you and the client, the agency can step in and mitigate the situation.

- **They act as your "salesperson."** Most agencies maintain a staff of salespeople who market the agency's services on a full-time basis. An agency is only as good as the people it hires or subcontracts. When the agency sells its services, it's also selling yours.

- **They get you in the door.** Some clients will only subcontract work to an agency that is an approved vendor. These clients believe this protects them from an IRS audit that could redefine subcontractors as their employees, forcing them to pay the IRS employee withholding taxes. If you really want to do work for a particular client with this restriction, you may have to do it through an agency.

Resources

The Want Ads

Search the business want ads in the section covering your area of expertise. Agencies and consulting companies often place ads when they are looking for professionals to complete a client project.

National Association of Computer Consultant Businesses

http://www.naccb.org

The NACCB is an association of agencies and consulting firms that hire consultants in the information technology (IT) industry. The site includes a search engine so you can search the member directory for IT agencies in your region. The membership includes agencies in Canada, Japan, the United Kingdom, and the United States.

22. Creatively cut your price

You will encounter other situations in which you may consider temporarily reducing your rates. The following are some basic situations in which you should consider reducing your rate.

- **Stimulate business during a slow cycle.** Your industry may experience seasonal cycles of feast and famine, and recessions are an economic fact. During slow periods you may want to offer a "seasonal discount" in which you offer a discount to new and existing clients for a specified time. To alert your current clients, you could send them an announcement about your special seasonal rate.

- **Target new clients.** New clients may hesitate to try a new business, so you could offer a "new client discount" rate. Another way you can target new clients is to publish coupons for product discounts or free hours of consultation. Make sure the client understands this is a "one-time only" offer and that your standard prices will kick in at some point.

- **Reward a loyal client.** You may want to offer a special discount or your wholesale rate to a client with whom you have a special relationship. There are several reasons why you might consider doing this. Perhaps the client has consistently patronized your business for a long time and you want to keep the client happy. Maybe you find a project particularly appealing even though the client can't budget for your full rate.

- **Regulate cash flow.** To encourage clients to hire you for longer periods, you may want to offer a "volume discount," in which you discount your rate if the client commits to a minimum number of hours. You can also offer a discount if the client prepays hours or hires you on a "retainer" basis. This is a win-win situation because you get your money up front and the client gets a discount or at least protection from a price increase.

The main goal is to lower your prices to attract new business without looking desperate. If your business hits tough times and you agree to take less to get the business without a clear plan on how this cut in revenues will affect your cash flow, your business could actually lose money. Also, you should never take less money without making it clear to your client that you are reducing the tasks, options, or perceived value of your service or product. Otherwise, you are only reducing your margin and the client or customer could assume that, because you are willing to deliver the same product at a reduced price, this is the price you could have and should have offered in the first place.

Here are some ideas for cutting your prices without looking desperate:

- **Reduce what you will deliver.** If you can, segment options or tasks in such a way that you can offer an "economy version" of your service or product by removing some value-added items. As a result, the client knows that there is value to these items and that you are willing to work within the budget. However, make sure that you don't "cut into the bone" of what you deliver.

- **Put a time limit on a discount.** If you discount your service or product, limit the length of your discount offer and direct the discount to new customers only. This limit encourages new clients to act now. This also creates a built-in shelf life for your discount so that you don't have discount offers with an unlimited time limit floating around when the demand (and the price) for your product and services rise in the future.

- **Show discounts on your invoice.** If you temporarily discount your price, the client might assume your price adjustment is permanent and forget the value of the lower price if you don't actually show it on your invoice. Print the full price on your invoice, followed by a line subtracting the discount amount, and then the final, lower amount. The client will see the savings with every invoice, and you can revert to your full price when appropriate, according to your contract.

- **Provide coupons.** Coupons with a time limit have additional advantages when they're used to attract new customers. If you require the original coupon, it's easier to trace how the prospect found out about your offering.

23. Offer "fixed bid" pricing

For many types of customizable work, clients prefer a "fixed bid" rather than a bill based on expended hours. Clients like this situation because it makes it easier for them to budget for the work. When you bid for a project based on a fixed bid, the client pays one price for the entire project regardless of how long it takes you to complete it. This is also called a "project fee." A typical scenario is to request one-third payment up front, one-third when a project milestone is reached, and final payment when the project is completed. The advantage is that if you work efficiently and complete the project according to your estimate or even ahead of schedule, you could make a larger profit than if you billed the same time on an hourly basis. The disadvantage is that if you do not meet your estimate you could end up working for a fraction of your hourly rate.

Fixed-bid projects work best when you control the design and delivery of the solution. For example, a standard repetitive procedure, such as conducting a survey you designed yourself, would be appropriate for fixed-bid projects. However, be wary of projects that depend on constantly changing technology. You may want to give a project estimate with a built-in reassessment period at specific checkpoints.

Increasing Your Credentials

Your credentials help define your personal brand. This is particularly true for free agents in the consulting field. You can build your credentials through education, formal certifications, and professional recognition. If you have a recognized degree, certification, or award, you will make that a part of your marketing materials. Credentials help customers build confidence in your abilities.

24. Finish your degree or start a new one

Degrees in your industry add to your qualifications. So if you started a degree some time ago and didn't finish it, consider completing the degree part time while you operate your business. If you believe your current educational background does not enhance your qualifications and your field is weighted heavily toward people with the proper education, working toward a formal degree may be time and money well invested. However, if you don't have the time and resources to obtain a regular degree, many fields provide shortened versions of fully advanced degrees as certificate programs.

Resources

Quintessential Careers

http://www.quintcareers.com

This website has a wealth of articles and tips on careers and advanced degrees. The site claims to have more than 1,600 pages of college, career, and job search content.

25. Become certified

Although certification isn't required in most fields, it enhances your qualifications. Many certification programs are either tied to an industry professional organization or particular industry products. Choosing the proper product certification can be a key part of your overall marketing plan, and in most cases, completing a product certification program is quicker and less expensive than enrolling in an advanced degree program at a university.

In some fields, such as medicine, law, or accounting, you cannot even practice without the proper certification. In many other fields, although certification isn't technically required, it becomes the "coin of the realm." For instance, if you intend to consult on computer network installation, you should become a Certified Network Engineer (CNE) in Novell or Microsoft networking products.

Microsoft maintains an extensive certified professional program for all its major products and provides limited marketing for its consultants. When you become a Microsoft certified consultant, in most cases, you earn the right to display the Microsoft certified consultant logo on your business card. This can be quite a selling point if you are marketing to Microsoft users. Many other technology products also provide certification programs particularly for consultants who train users in their product. Other examples from the software industry are Quark, Adobe, and Power Builder.

The technology field isn't the only one that provides certification programs. For many other fields there are professional organizations or products that sponsor certification programs. For example, ISO 9000 is a set of international guidelines intended to evaluate a company's ability to respond to quality issues. Some companies, particularly in Europe, require their vendors to be ISO 9000 compliant. So there are certification programs for consultants that can help companies get ISO 9000 status.

Next time you see a business card or advertisement for someone offering consulting services in your field, look for any certification logos and find out what the requirements are to get certified.

Resources

Get Certified and Get Ahead, Millennium Edition

by Anne Martinez. New York: McGraw-Hill, ISBN 0070411271. This book provides information about more than 170 computer certifications including A+, Adobe, C++, Certified Computing Professional (CCP), Certified Internet Webmaster, Cisco, Microsoft, Novell, Power Builder, Java, Lotus, SAP, Visual Basic, and more. It also provides listings of websites, books, magazines, and information on more than 40 vendors of preparation materials to help you get certified.

Certification **Magazine**

http://www.certmag.com
This site is maintained by MediaTec Publishing, Inc., which publishes *Certification* and *IT Contractor* magazines. The publication and the website list IT professionals, technical trainers, and companies that develop or deliver certification programs and training. Feature stories focus on certification trends, events and happenings, regular reviews of courseware and training resources, and interviews with industry leaders. The publication also provides updates of requirements for certification programs.

Transcender

http://www.transcender.com
This site sells self-study and simulation software to prepare for Microsoft certification exams.

Brainbench

http://www.brainbench.com
Brainbench assessments enable members to earn certifications in more than 425 of today's leading skills, and new subjects are added regularly. Brainbench assessments employ computer adaptive testing technology developed under strict ISO 9001 standards. The assessments include a job role certification program in which job roles were developed by using the O*NET classification system of the U.S. Department of Labor

and Brainbench subject matter experts. Complete job role certifications include core skills as well as "elective" skills you can choose based on your specific needs. Membership in Brainbench is free, and most tests are nominally priced.

GoCertify

http://www.gocertify.com

GoCertify is an online resource for certification information: certification descriptions, costs, requirements, perks, contact information, and more. The site provides information on more than 500 certifications from more than 90 vendors.

Certiport

http://www.certiport.com

Certiport, Inc. is the exclusive worldwide provider of the Microsoft Office User Specialist (MOUS) program. It also administers the more generic Computing Core Certification (IC³). The site features a searchable database of certification centers (called "iQcenters") so you can find the nearest location where you can take the tests. The site also sells preparation CDs for the certifications it administers.

Techies.com

http://www.techies.com

This job site focuses on information technology (IT) professionals. In addition to job searches, the site includes articles and links for IT training and certification programs.

26. Enter your work in a competition

Industry awards help distinguish you from your competition, particularly in a field in which clients have trouble judging the difference between good and bad practitioners. For example, in the field of technical communication (i.e., technical writing), many clients have trouble judging the nuances of good and bad documentation. Fortunately, every year the Society for Technical Communication (STC) sponsors a technical publications competition. Being an "award winner" in any field is a concept any client can understand and differentiates you from your competition.

The following are some potential sources of competitions:

- **Professional organizations.** The best place to look for competitions is professional organizations for your field. If your field produces something that can be judged, it may have a competition to acknowledge the best examples of work produced in the industry. Even if the organization does not hold a competition, you can get involved with the organization by volunteering and being recognized for your contribution through a service award.

- **Local business organizations.** Local chambers of commerce or business associations often have "entrepreneur of the year" awards or "most socially responsible company" awards. Find out what the requirements are and work toward getting nominated for one of these awards.

- **website design competitions.** If you think your website is "smokin'," you can enter in a Web design competition.

Resources

Here are some organizations that give Web design awards:

Webby Awards
http://www.webbyawards.com

Golden Globe Awards
http://www.goldenwebawards.com

WebMaster Award
http://www.marketme.com/awards

Best of the Web Awards
http://www.websiteawards2.cjb.net

27. Gain professional recognition

Many professional organizations have fellowship or other programs that recognize outstanding contributions to their field. Many of the activities you should be doing to network in your field are the same activities that may get you nominated for professional recognition.

The following are some common activities that may get you noticed:

- Write articles for an organization's professional journal
- Run for a position as an officer in the organization
- Volunteer to run a committee
- Teach a seminar for the organization
- Volunteer to present a program at a meeting
- Represent the organization at a trade show
- Mentor a peer in your profession.

Marketing from Your Home Office

"Here is a pen and here is a pencil,
Here's a typewriter, here's a stencil,
Here is a list of today's appointments,
And all the flies in all the ointments,
The daily woes that a man endures —
Take them, George, they're yours!"

—Ogden Nash (1902–71), U.S. poet. *Let George Do It, If You Can Find Him*, in *The Primrose Path* (1935).

As a free agent, you are likely to conduct most of your marketing from your home office. The goal for setting up a home office is to create an efficient workspace separate from your private life so that when you are on the phone with clients, family members cannot easily interrupt you.

Today's technology helps make the home office an ideal communications center for your marketing efforts. From your home, you can have efficient access to voice and digital connections. It's easier and less expensive to add toll-free numbers and credit card merchant accounts than in years past. Telecommunication companies provide built-in telephone options that, years ago, would have required expensive PBX equipment installed on your premises. There's even a new way to add a "fax machine" to your office without purchasing a physical device of any kind.

49

28. Maximize your outgoing voice mail message

You probably use an automated answering system to take messages when you cannot answer the phone. Rather than using your outgoing message only to identify yourself, use it to sell your business. Your introduction can include a snippet about your business and your credentials. Consider occasionally changing your outgoing message so it doesn't get stale and you don't bore regular callers. You could include updates on company news, special offers, or even a quote from a famous person.

Here's an example of how you can spruce up your outgoing voice mail message to feature your business:

Instead of:

"Thank you for calling ABC Consulting. Please leave your message at the beep."

Record this:

"Welcome to ABC Consulting, award-winning designers of commercial websites and certified web trainers. Let us design an efficient, affordable, website for your company that gets results. You've reached the voice mail of Toby Powers. I cannot answer your call right now, but if you leave a message, it will receive my prompt attention."

29. Obtain a toll-free number

One way to encourage customers to call you, regardless of their location, is to get a toll-free number. It would be nice to get the traditional "800" area code, but because those numbers are used up, telecommunications vendors now issue other area codes for toll-free access. Nonetheless, it works the same way, and because of competition, the cost of getting a toll-free line is comparatively low.

There are two ways you can add toll-free access to your business. You can add a live toll-free line that forwards calls to your business line, or you can add an automated message system with a toll-free phone number. To add a live toll-free line, contact one of the telecommunications companies such as ATT, Sprint, or Verizon. To add a toll-free message system, contact any vendor, such as eFax.com. Typically, if someone calls the toll-free message system, they hear your outgoing message and leave a voice message for you that you can retrieve by phone or even have automatically sent to your e-mail address as a digital audio file.

Resources

All the major telecommunications carriers offer toll-free service. Here's a few:

ATT

(877) 490-1971

http://www.att.com

Sprint

(800) 370-6105

http://www.sprint.com

Verizon

http://www.verizon.com

eFax

www.eFax.com

For a monthly fee, eFax offers a dedicated toll-free number answering system on which callers can leave a message. The phone number also accepts faxes (see below). eFax delivers the message to you as an audio file attached to an e-mail message. However, to listen to a voice message, you have to use the free eFax software that is provided when you sign up.

30. Add a fax machine in 5 minutes!

Want to send and receive faxes without the hassle of maintaining a fax machine and adding another phone line to your house? Sign up for an Internet fax service. Here's how it works: you open an account and a fax phone number is assigned to you. You can put this number on your letterhead, business cards, website—anywhere you would normally display your fax number. The number connects into the fax service's system, but to the rest of the world it works the same as if you had a fax machine connected to your own private line.

When you receive a fax, the fax system digitizes the fax image and sends it to you as a digital picture that you can open, read, and print using software supplied by the fax vendor. When you want to send a fax, you compose your document in a word processor and attach it to an e-mail you send to an address supplied by the fax service. If you need to send an image of something like a printed photograph or a newspaper clipping, you will have to scan these items and attach the digital image to your e-mail. Once the fax service receives your e-mail, it faxes your document or image to the recipient you indicate in the e-mail.

One major advantage of this system over a traditional fax machine is that it is paperless. You don't have to print out the faxes you receive to read them and you can maintain a database consisting of digital images of all the faxes you receive. Unlike paper files, this electronic version takes up no physical space in your filing cabinet.

Resources

eFax
http://www.eFax.com
For a monthly fee, eFax offers a dedicated local or toll-free fax number. The fax number doubles as a voice message system. People can leave voice messages using your eFax number and the message is delivered to you as an audio file attached to an e-mail message. However, to read a fax or listen to a voice message, you have to use the free eFax software.

31. Accept credit cards

If you sell a physical product, you should definitely consider accepting credit cards. Even if you are a consulting or service company, you should consider accepting credit card payments from your customers. For any type of business, there are many advantages to accepting credit cards:

- **Point-of-sale convenience.** If you are personally hand-selling physical product to your customers, credit cards provide speedy and convenient transactions.
- **International currency.** If you do business remotely with customers or clients in another country, the credit card company handles all the currency conversions. While this service is an obvious advantage to a store that sells a physical product, it can also be used by one company to pay a consulting company in another country.

- **Quick payment.** You get paid by the credit card company quickly, usually by an electronic funds transfer directly into your company bank account.

- **Payment insurance.** The credit card company acts as guarantor and referee for the transaction. You get guaranteed payment from the credit card company and the client has the ability to protest an inappropriate charge.

You can accept credit cards directly or indirectly. When you accept credit cards directly, you either physically handle the customer's credit card or receive the credit card number via phone, fax, or website. You are required to have a merchant account with a credit card service. The credit card service can be through your bank or an independent service. With a merchant account, the service company charges a fixed monthly fee and a transaction fee on any credit card sales. Transaction fees can be a percentage of the sale or a combination fixed fee and percentage. Transaction percentages are typically 2%–6%. The service company also sells you a transaction machine, or you can purchase one on your own. These are the small devices that store clerks use to swipe your card for a purchase. When you get a transaction machine, the credit card service programs it to work with their system. When you handle the customer's credit card or number, you have to enter or swipe their number into the transaction machine to complete the transaction.

When you indirectly accept credit card payments over the Internet, your customer enters the credit card information on a secure site and a third party service verifies the card and handles the transaction; you don't see the customer's credit card number. The advantages to using an online credit card service are twofold. First, the requirements for starting an account are usually less stringent than those for opening a merchant account. Second, you don't have to purchase a transaction machine.

Resources

Charge.com

http://www.charge.com

This site provides a means to sign up for a merchant account so you can accept credit cards such as Visa and MasterCard for your business. Charge.com claims to be the number one credit card merchant account provider on the Internet.

PayPal

http://www.PayPal.com.

PayPal handles electronic payments on the Internet. The company has an option in which you can accept online credit card payments from individuals even if they are not members of PayPal.

32. Accept Internet payments

With the growth of online auction sites like eBay, the need for an efficient, safe, and quick means of electronic payment has increased. Several transaction service websites have stepped in to fill this need. Some of these websites, such as PayPal, require you to actually create an online bank account with them, into and out of which you transfer money to and from your regular bank accounts. Others, such as eBay's BillPoint electronically transfer funds from the buyer's credit card or checking account to the seller's bank account.

In either case, these services extract a transaction fee from the seller similar to the way a merchant account extracts a transaction fee for credit card transactions. However, Internet payment sites often offer better rates than merchant accounts. PayPal's merchant rate is 2.2% plus $0.30 per transaction.

Typically buyers can pay in three ways: Internet payment account, credit cards, or electronic check. If they have an account on a service like PayPal, they can pay directly from the funds in that account by indicating the e-mail address of the person they want to pay. Recipients also have to be members of the same service. If buyers use credit cards, their purchase is debited from their credit card in the same manner as for any other credit card purchase. Electronic check acts like a debit card. It allows the buyer to pay online by entering their account number and usually providing a secondary form of identification. Then the Internet payment service transfers funds directly from the buyer's checking account.

Resources

PayPal

http://www.PayPal.com

Recently purchased by eBay, this electronic "bank" is very popular with people who auction items on eBay. PayPal provides an efficient way to send money electronically via the Internet. To use PayPal, you establish a

PayPal electronic bank account into which you transfer funds for purchases. You can link your PayPal account to any of your regular checking accounts. Currently, PayPal is paying a competitive interest rate for funds kept in a PayPal account with no minimum balance. When someone uses PayPal to pay you, PayPal extracts a small transaction fee from the proceeds and electronically deposits the net funds in your PayPal account. People who pay you can be other PayPal members or you can use PayPal HTML code to allow non-PayPal members to order merchandise on your website using major credit cards.

Billpoint.com

http://billpoint.com

BillPoint is a fully owned subsidiary of eBay. Although it's primarily used by people to accept payments for eBay auctions, the service also offers the ability to use BillPoint to accept payments anywhere on the Internet. When you use BillPoint for eBay auctions, you use it in conjunction with eBay payments to register and list your items with a payment method. Then buyers can pay with a credit card or checking account directly from the item listing. Unlike PayPal, you do not maintain a bank account with BillPoint. BillPoint extracts a transaction fee and moves the money from buyers to sellers using electronic direct deposit of funds into the seller's bank account. The seller specifies the bank account to be used for BillPoint when enrolling with the service.

Yahoo! PayDirect

http://paydirect.yahoo.com

PayDirect is Yahoo's service to send or receive money online. Similar to PayPal, when you sign up for Yahoo! PayDirect, you are opening an online bank account. You can transfer money between your online account and your regular bank account. Once set up, your Yahoo! PayDirect account can be used to send money to anyone in the United States. who has an e-mail address. To do this, you provide a name and e-mail address, along with the amount you are sending. PayDirect sends the recipient an e-mail notifying them that money is waiting at Yahoo! PayDirect. To receive the money, the recipient must already have an existing Yahoo! PayDirect account or open a new PayDirect account.

The "Group Billing" feature allows you to simultaneously request money from more than one person. For example, if you were a travel agent and you organized a cruise or ski trip for a club, you can send bills to all group members with one click. You can monitor the status of your collections through PayDirect, and you receive an e-mail notifying you of each payment.

C2it

http://www.c2it.com

C2it is a Citibank service that allows you to move money to and from your bank account or credit card to anyone within the United States as well as to more than 100 countries. Similar to BillPoint, you do not have to have an account with C2it or Citibank to use this service. You can use any U.S.-based checking, savings, and/or money market accounts. You can also use any MasterCard or Visa credit card accounts, but currently you cannot use MasterCard and Visa debit cards to receive cash. To retrieve cash, recipients have to enroll in C2it. Once they do, they can send the money to someone else domestically or internationally, transfer it to any of their linked bank or credit card accounts, or request a paper check. Currently, C2it lets you send, receive and move money within the U.S. for free. When you use C2it to send money internationally, the charge is $10 per international check and $10 per international direct deposit.

33. Obtain a broadband connection

With the competition between digital subscriber line (DSL) and cable providers increasing every year, the cost of a broadband connection is coming down. In contrast to a standard 56K modem, a broadband connection provides a faster connection to the Internet and is always "on" (i.e., you don't have to dial up).

Although there are other exotic implementations of broadband connections such as satellite, wireless, and fiber optics, the two most prevalent right now are DSL and cable. DSL uses standard twisted pair telephone line that is probably already installed in your home. Cable Internet connections use a coaxial cable connection like the one for your cable TV. Both types of connections require a specialized modem that the provider supplies or is often available at a computer store. There are many industry arguments about which is better (cable or DSL), but either type of connection will provide an advantage over a 56K dial-up modem. Your choice will be largely determined by the vendors available in your area.

How does a broadband connection translate into a marketing tool? By having a broadband connection, you can access your e-mail, view websites, maintain your own website, and transfer files to your customers more quickly than your 56K-modem-equipped competition. A broadband connection not only saves you a great deal of time, but also can be a part of your Unique Selling Proposition (USP). In your marketing materials you can point out that you can maintain better customer service because you have a broadband connection. This is particularly important if you are a technology consultant (Web designer, graphic designer, programmer, technical writer) or someone whose main product is information.

Resources

Broadband Reports

http://www.dslreports.com

The type of broadband connection (if any) available to you is determined by the vendors servicing your area. Before you select a broadband service, you may want to visit this website. You can list all the services available in your area based on your zip code. You can read industry news and reviews of services written by broadband subscribers. You can use their tools to test the speed of your connection and maintain an online "connection diary."

Using the Power of Networking

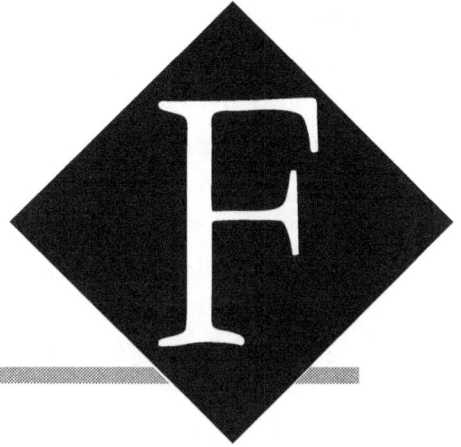

"I look upon every day to be lost, in which I do not make a new acquaintance."

—Samuel Johnson (1709–84), English author, lexicographer. Quoted in: James Boswell, *Life of Samuel Johnson*, Nov. 1784 (1791).

Networking could be your best marketing technique. Networking is a somewhat subtle art that probably lies somewhere between casual conversation and outright promotion or salesmanship. The primary method of networking is talking one-on-one to someone in person or over the phone.

You already have access to many different networks. In addition to professional organizations, there are family, friends, ex-employees, ex-employers, vendors, professionals (accountant, lawyer, doctor), former schoolmates, and neighbors, to name a few.

There are two ways to network: random networking and targeted networking. With random networking you try to meet as many people as possible to find out what they do and how you can work with them. With targeted networking, you determine whom you need to know and find someone who can introduce you to those people or identify where you can find them.

Go to forums sponsored by professional organizations, conventions, classrooms, seminars, and basically any place where people in your field congregate. However, don't attend only the same events as your colleagues. One of the best ways to network to find more clients is to attend events at which potential clients tend to gather. Go where your clients are—product release seminars, trade shows, industry functions, etc.

Here are some tips for networking.

Do's

- **Continue networking when you're busy.** As with all your marketing activities, you must continue networking even when business is good.

- **Dress appropriately.** Dress right for the occasion. Wear business attire for a program meeting or convention; dress casual for a picnic; wear business or casual clothing for a class or seminar.

- **Always carry your business cards with you.** At a minimum, be ready to give out your business card if someone asks for it. You might also want to have a copy of your resume and/or brochure. You may not want to offer these last two items right away, unless the person you are talking to specifically asks for them.

- **Ask people about their business.** Their conversation not only keeps you from always talking about yourself, but also provides you with information about their business situation.

- **Write notes on the back of other people's business cards.** If someone requested more information about your business, write what they wanted on the back of their card. Also write down where you met them and the date.

- **Volunteer to help.** One of the best ways to network is to volunteer to assist the organization with which you do most of your networking. This gives you a higher profile in the organization, allows you to meet with organization insiders, and builds your credentials.

Don'ts

- **Don't focus only about yourself.** Listening is the most important input for your business. Pace yourself, let the other person talk, and pay attention!

- **Don't become a "black hole."** A black hole sucks all the energy in and gives nothing back. Don't use networking to get free consulting on how to run your business or to pump someone for referrals.

- **Don't complain.** No one wants to hear someone whine about how badly they need new business. You won't get business by trying to make people feel sorry for you.

- **Don't "push" marketing materials.** Don't walk up to a stranger with one hand extended for a handshake and the other hand holding your business card and resume. If someone wants to know how to reach you or get more information, you will get some indication or they will ask for it. Wait for the right signal.

- **Avoid discussing politics or religion with someone you don't know well.** Unless you are networking at a political or religious forum with like-minded people, it's best to hold off expressing your stand on these issues until you get to know the person better.

34. Join professional organizations

The most accessible form of networking is the professional organization appropriate for your industry. With thousands of professional organizations available, you can probably find one with a local chapter that has meetings close to you. In addition to networking, these organizations often offer many other benefits including directory listings, training, publications, books, health plans, insurance, and discounts on office supplies and services.

In addition to networking in organizations of your peers, you might consider joining organizations at whose meetings you might find your clients. For example, a programmer who is a member of the Independent Computer Consultants Association (ICCA) may also join the Association of Information Technology Professionals (AITP), Software Publishers Association (SPA), and the Association for Systems Management (ASM). Even if you do not qualify to join an alternative organization directly, you can usually attend their regularly scheduled program meetings as a nonmember.

In Practice

Jennifer Berkley credits much of her success to networking. She's owner of The Insight Advantage, a San Jose, California consulting company that provides customer research, including surveys, interviews, and focus groups. "I have built up a reputation for the work I do over the past two years primarily via networking. I selected a few groups that best fit my needs. This allows me to rub elbows with my target market and become a regular in all of them. I also volunteer in over half of them," she says.

Berkley has a specific strategy for networking. "I always follow up with people I have met at meetings. This makes an impression with people. I also look for other ways to make an impression by sharing other resources to

help people in their businesses, sending them news of interest, and so forth."
She also believes in quality versus quantity in her networking. "I focus on three
good interactions versus ten quickie ones," she says.

Berkley figures she spent about $1,000 in membership fees to do net-
working. "The results are beginning to pay off with referrals coming from
people I don't even know who heard about me from someone else. Keeping
in touch after the initial contact definitely pays off in the long run!"

Resources

Successful Independent

http://www.SuccessfulIndependent.com
This website, maintained by this book's publisher, includes a list of professional organizations that are either designed for free agents and
independent consultants or include special interest groups (SIGs) that
focus on specific industries.

Association Central

http://www.AssociationCentral.com
This site provides a free, searchable online database of nearly 40,000
trade associations, professional societies, affinity organizations, and other
nonprofit groups.

Free Agent Forum

http://www.FreeAgentForum.com.
This group in the New York City area sponsors regular meetings called
Social Capitalism™. These meetings are described as "an innovative
method for structured networking where we match you up with Free
Agents that complement your work and your life." In addition to networking, members can win prizes at Social Capitalism meetings. One-day
seasonal conferences feature experts on Free Agency, journalists, financial
managers, and marketing and sales gurus. Membership plans start at $125.

Free Agent Nation

http://www.FreeAgentNation.com
This site is maintained by Daniel Pink, former speechwriter for Vice
President Al Gore and author of the book *Free Agent Nation*. In addition
to articles and newsletters by Pink, you can find out about his networking

concept called Free Agent Nation (FAN) clubs. He defines these as "clusters of free agents who meet regularly to offer support and exchange business advice." Subscribers to the website are encouraged to start and promote their local FAN club through FreeAgentNation.com.

Fast Company of Friends (CoF)

http://www.fastcompany/cof

The website for *Fast Company* magazine is loaded with excellent articles for independent professionals and small-business owners, including some that are exclusive to FastCompany.com. Membership in the Company of Friends (CoF) network is free. CoF maintains local chapters in the United States and throughout the world. These chapters have regular meetings for networking with other professionals. Members can also download PDF versions of articles from the magazine. Daniel Pink and Seth Godin are regular contributors, and their articles from the magazine are available on this website.

Dig Your Well Before You're Thirsty: The Only Networking Book You'll Ever Need

by Harvey Mackay. New York: Doubleday, 1999, ISBN 0385485468.
This book is written by the best-selling author of *Swim with the Sharks*. He reveals his techniques for networking including finding and starting networks, culling your list of contacts, tracking favors, and coaching for "small talk."

Encyclopedia of Associations

Kimberly N. Hunt (Editor). Gale Group, 39th ed., 2002,
ISBN 0787648299.
This publication is rather expensive, so check your local library for this three volume set. It contains information about nearly 23,000 national and international organizations. The following are some of the categories: trade, business, commercial, environmental, agricultural, legal, government, public administration, military, engineering, technology, sciences, educational, cultural, social welfare, health and medical, public affairs, fraternal, ethnic, religious, veterans, hereditary, patriotic, hobby, vocational, athletic, labor unions, chambers of commerce, tourism, fraternities, sororities, and fan clubs. It provides detailed information about each organization including address, phone and fax numbers, e-mail address,

website URL, publications (directories, magazines, newsletters, and the like), conventions and meetings, and awards.

Directory of National Trade and Professional Associations of the United States

by Buck Downs (Editor). Columbia Books Inc., 37th ed., 2001, ISBN 1880873478.

Check this publication to find appropriate trade and professional organizations that regularly conduct conferences for their members and those that provide an exhibit area at their conference.

35. Acquire a mentor

If you're struggling with your business or planning a major expansion and you don't have enough money to interest a business consultant, consider getting a mentor for your business. In most cases, mentors are other business owners who want to give back something to their communities by helping other fledgling companies. Mentoring is a one-on-one relationship between a financial, legal, or other professional and you.

The mentoring relationship can take many forms. You can build a "board of directors" comprising several interested mentors with whom you meet regularly. You can meet with a mentor at a business organization such as the Small Business Administration (SBA), Service Corps of Retired Executtives (SCORE), or a local small-business development center.

Resources

Small Business Development Centers

http://www.sba.gov/sbdc

The SBA site provides links to all the 58 Small Business Development Centers (SBDCs) in every state (Texas has four), the District of Columbia, Guam, Puerto Rico, Samoa, and the U.S. Virgin Islands. The SBA administers the Small Business Development Center Program to provide management assistance to current and prospective small business owners. SBDCs offer one-stop assistance to small businesses by providing a wide variety of information and guidance in central and easily accessible branch locations.

Each center has a director, staff members, volunteers, and part-time personnel. Qualified individuals recruited from professional and trade associations, the legal and banking community, academia, chambers of commerce, and SCORE are among those who donate their services. SBDCs also use paid consultants, consulting engineers and testing laboratories from the private sector to help clients who need specialized expertise.

SCORE

http://www.score.org

SCORE is specifically chartered to be "counselors to America's small business" by the SBA. SCORE has more than 11,500 volunteer business counselors providing small business mentoring and advice on a full range of business topics. At this website, you can find a SCORE chapter in your local community so you can meet with a SCORE counselor face-to-face or can receive free and confidential business advice via e-mail.

Guerrilla Marketing Association

http://www.guerrillamarketingassociation.com

This site is operated by Jay Conrad Levinson, author of the "Guerrilla Marketing" series of books. For a monthly fee, this site provides a small business support group that helps its members increase their profits with Guerrilla Marketing tactics and techniques. Membership benefits include a Marketing Coaching Forum and a weekly interactive telephone Q&A session.

36. "Buy" time with a prospect

One creative way to do targeted networking is to attend charity functions that auction a lunch with a business leader. If you win the bid, you have access to the corporate officer of a major company in a way that you could never get otherwise. Depending on the bidding, the cost could be less than that for direct mail or other forms of advertising to try and get in front of a busy executive. Besides, you are doing a good thing by contributing to a charity.

If these kinds of auctions are not available in your area, why not start one? Suggest to your professional organization that it sponsor such an event. Even better, offer to organize it. This way, you get to recruit the business leaders who are willing to be auctioned and also participate in the auction when it's held.

In Practice

When Nancy Michaels, co-author of *Off the Wall Marketing* and owner of Impression Impact, arrived at a Success Strategies for Business Women Conference in Boca Raton, Florida, she didn't know that she was about to get a fantastic marketing opportunity. By the end of the day, she was going to get a shot at pitching her business ideas to the CEO of Office Depot.

While attending the conference, Michaels was excited to find out that the conference sponsor, Office Depot, was auctioning a lunch with chairman and CEO Bruce Nelson and donating the proceeds to Count-Me-In, a women's nonprofit organization. Realizing the value of a chance to meet with a key decision maker in an industry familiar to her, Michaels seized the moment. "I had my American Express card and decided I would bid as high as $1,000," she says. Her plan was to win the silent auction and pitch her idea to have Office Depot host in-store marketing seminars for small businesses. So she waited until the last 10 minutes of the silent auction to put in her bid, but was surprised to see an existing bid of $1,000. Determined to win the auction despite her self-imposed $1,000 limit, Michaels increased the bid to $1,050 and won the auction.

"It was the most expensive lunch I ever bought," she says. Although risky, her gambit paid off. She was able to interest Nelson in a pilot program for her small-business seminars. "People like to do business with someone they know and trust and this was a great way to gain access," Nancy says. Although $1,050 seems like a lot of money, Michaels saw other benefits even if Office Depot wasn't interested in her ideas. As she puts it, "This was a great opportunity to make a connection while contributing to a worthy cause."

37. Attend product release seminars

One way you can gain access to prospects is to attend seminars for products sold to your client base. Product release or product rollout seminars are frequently conducted by software companies such as Microsoft and Macromedia. However, look for any product vendor that has a product that you or clients are most likely to use. These events are usually free, and they offer a great opportunity to network with potential clients.

When you attend one of these events, check those nametags! Your prospecting at any networking event should not be confined to the presentation itself. Often the event organizers leave the nametags of people who registered for the event out on the registration table. After the presentation starts, the registration table is often unattended. On your way out, make note of the names and companies listed on the unused nametags.

Resources

Microsoft Events Homepage

http://msevents.microsoft.com
Microsoft conducts product seminars throughout the world, many of which are business specific. Check this website to determine whether there is an appropriate event in your area.

38. Attend trade shows

Trade shows offer an opportunity to meet with potential clients; you can exhibit at the trade show or be an attendee and keep your ears open for opportunities. Trade shows offer the opportunity to network with other attendees, but it's possible the show's exhibitors could be potential clients. At larger trade shows, it's common for an industry leader to host a cocktail party or other networking event, providing you with another opportunity to meet potential clients.

Resources

Expo World

http://www.expoworld.net
The Las Vegas Conventions and Visitors Authority hosts this site where you can search for events by industry, country, or world region.

Chicago Conventions

http://www.mccormickplace.com
Chicago is host to many conventions, trade shows, and expositions. Check the schedule of this website to search for events by name.

39. Attend professional conferences

Another value of professional organizations is that the larger ones host conferences providing excellent opportunities to network with others in your field. These events usually include educational seminars that help you stay sharp in your profession. In addition to attending professional conferences for your field, you should consider attending or exhibiting at a conference your clients are likely to attend. Many conferences include a vendor exhibition area where you can register to set up a booth. These conference exhibition areas are typically smaller and less expensive than trade shows.

40. Attend career fairs

Job or career fairs offer another marketing opportunity, particularly for independent consultants, free agents, and contractors. Check the job section of your local paper or popular job sites for any mention of job or career fairs for your industry. These events offer you the chance to talk with companies that need additional resources for their business.

Prepare a short resume and/or list of successfully completed projects. Make sure you place on your resume, somewhere near the top in bold type, the words "Contract _____ (insert the term for your profession)." For example, if you're a technical writer, you would insert "Contract Technical Writer." You don't want your resume to be confused with those applying for a permanent position in the company. Your goal is not necessarily to get a project right away, but to make contact with companies and get information about your services into their hands, so that when the need arises, they can contact you.

Try to get a list of the companies that will exhibit at the career fair, and then target the companies you want to contact. For example, you may decide you don't want to talk with any agencies, preferring to develop more direct clients. Make sure you give yourself plenty of time to speak with all your target companies. Exhibiting companies typically spend the last half hour of the last day of a career fair packing up their materials and breaking down their display, so they will not be available to talk. When you introduce yourself, explain that you are a free agent and you wish to offer your services on a contract basis.

When you introduce yourself, you will get one of several reactions:

- **"We don't hire contractors."** Some companies have strict policies of never hiring contractors, only permanent employees. In this case, all you can do is thank them and move on to another booth.

- **"Are you interested in a permanent position?"** Don't be surprised if a company tries to lure you into a permanent position. As an expert independent consultant, you're a good catch for a company looking to hire the best. Of course, you can always consider this, but if you are truly committed to your independent consulting business, you should be flattered and politely explain you would like to remain independent for now. Some companies have a difficult time filling permanent positions when there is a shortage of people available with a particular skill. Sometimes this holds up completion of a particular project. If this is the case, you can suggest they consider hiring you to keep the project moving forward while they continue to search for a permanent employee. You can even offer to help them find a qualified candidate as an additional, value-added service while you work on the project.

- **"I'm not sure where to submit your resume."** One disadvantage of career fairs from a free agent's point of view is that when you go to the booth of a larger company, you will probably talk to someone from the human resources (HR) department. Because these events are usually organized with the intention of acquiring a permanent employee, the HR departments of some companies often don't know how to handle resumes from contractors. When I introduce myself, I sometimes get a blank stare as the person operating the booth tries to figure out what "channel" in the company should receive the resume. If you know your industry well enough, you can usually suggest specific departments to which the HR person can submit your resume. This is much less of a problem with small and medium-sized companies that don't have HR departments; the CEO may even be the company's representative at the booth. These companies are usually very receptive to a resume from a free agent even if they don't have any current needs for your services.

- **"We don't currently have a need for a contractor."** Even if a company does not have a current need for your business, explain that you want to make them aware of your services should they need you in the future. Most companies who do not have a restriction against contractors will include your resume in their files.

Resources

NAACP High Tech and Diversity Job Fairs
http://www.naacpjobfair.com
Sponsored by the NAACP, this site provides listings of diversity career fairs across the United States.

41. Use a custom nametag

Whenever you attend a networking event, the person at the registration desk typically gives you the same boring nametag as everyone else. Who says you have to use their nametag? Why not create a custom nametag and use it at all your networking events? By creating your own nametag, you have a chance to create something that will stand out and spark conversation.

The following are a few tips for creating a custom nametag:

- Self-adhesive nametags tend to curl up at the corners. Use a plastic, clip-on nametag holder with an inserted nametag card.

- If possible, include some color in your nametag, but use it tastefully.

- Try to come up with a phrase that represents your USP (Unique Selling Proposition) and put this on your nametag. For example, you could include a question on your nametag such as "Ask me about…"

Resources

Avery
http://www.Avery.com
To find name badge supplies, visit your local office supply store or Avery's website.

42. Participate in beta product tests

If you operate a consulting business, particularly in the IT industry, consider participating in beta tests for products that affect either your business or the business of your clients. Beta product tests are prevalent for many software products, but some of your vendors may have physical products that they might want you to try out so they can work out the kinks. Here are the advantages of participating in beta product tests:

- You have the opportunity to network with other beta testers. This is more prevalent in software beta tests, but it could also apply to physical products. When software companies conduct a beta test, they often set up an e-mail discussion group or e-mail list for all the beta testers. This provides an opportunity to do some advertising for your business through your e-mail signature during the course of correspondence regarding issues raised about the product. You can also get an idea of what type of businesses are represented by the other beta testers through their e-mail signatures.

- It keeps you abreast of new technology. You can get a heads up on changes to products and/or software. This includes not only upgrades to software or products you currently use but also new products that could allow you to add a new revenue stream to your business.

- You get free support. During a beta test, you often have direct access to the product's designers, allowing you to ask questions that you might normally pay customer support to answer about a product.

Review software and product vendors that are strategic to you and your customer base. Call, write, or send e-mails to these companies to let them know you want to participate in the next beta test of their product.

43. Create cross-business promotions

Perhaps you can enter into a mutual system of referrals with a complementary business. For example, a programmer can refer a technical writer. A technical writer can refer graphic artists, indexers, and trainers and vice versa. You can also form an alliance with suppliers or even your clients to offer a "combo" package that none of you could offer alone. This type of alliance spreads the marketing expenses among all the members of the group. For example, an attorney can create a combined package of services with the accountant who prepares her taxes.

Make sure any agreement with another business is fair and balanced. You don't want to take on a second job of being the salesperson for another business and getting nothing in return. Make sure you are selecting a complementary business—not some generic consumer business that is trying to pump you for your client list. It makes sense for a programmer and technical writer to refer business to each other; however, a programmer and a party planner is not necessarily a good match. Technically, everyone the programmer meets is a potential client for the insurance salesperson, but the insurance salesperson will rarely meet someone who needs commercial programming services unless he or she specializes in selling insurance to software companies.

To find other businesses appropriate for cross-promotion, check your contact list for complementary businesses with which you have worked on a client project or whose services you have used yourself. Also attend some meetings at your local chamber of commerce to network and determine whether there are some complementary businesses that might be interested in cross-promotion.

Marketing Through Cold Calling

"In Hell all the messages you ever left on answering machines will be played back to you."

—Judy Horacek (b. 1961), Australian cartoonist.
Life on the Edge (1992).

Cold calling is a sales activity in which you personally contact a prospect who does not know you and attempt to sell them your product or services. You can do cold calling over the phone or show up in person at your prospect's place of business. However, you will most likely do your cold calling over the phone.

No one likes cold calling. Even veteran salespeople avoid it, preferring to sell to their existing customers instead. There is something about the repetitive rejection characteristic of cold calling that triggers the "fight or flight" response in most people.

Cold calling does, however, produce results. It is one marketing activity that allows you to actively try to get business and can produce results quickly if you hit the right prospect. Remember, somewhere out there, right at this moment, there is a manager, buyer, or owner sitting at his or her desk with a problem that your product or service can solve. They're waiting for your call! The smartest way to approach cold calling is to accept that you will dislike the experience and arm yourself with good strategies.

73

44. Conduct "warm calling"

You don't have to start with a list of contacts you don't know. Do some "warm calling" first. Try calling your former clients to see how they're doing. It's possible they are so busy trying to put out fires that they haven't had time to call for help, and you may contact them at the right time. You should be doing this form of customer service anyway, especially because repeat business is easier to get than new business.

45. Conduct local cold calling in person

Although telephone cold calling is probably more efficient, don't discount the potential for face-to-face cold calling. Sometimes it is easier to form a human bond in person so that you can use nonverbal body language and physical mannerisms to make a point. You also have the opportunity to appeal to prospects visually with brochures and your business card in a way that you cannot do over the phone.

Here are some tips for in-person cold calling:

- **Start close to home.** Because cold calling in person may require multiple visits, it's more efficient to start with prospects close to your home base. If you are visiting a customer in an office building or industrial park, look around. What other businesses can you call on in the area? The fact that you are already working with another business in the same building or complex is an ice breaker. You can introduce yourself by saying "I'm working with ABC company on the fourth floor and I noticed your business as I was passing by…"

- **Do reconnaissance first.** You don't have to have a meeting with the decision maker right away. Ask the receptionist for information about what the business sells. Study these materials to get the decision maker's name and to research any problems in the operation for which you can provide a solution. Then come back and make a pitch to see the decision maker. Of course, you can do reconnaissance by studying the company website (assuming there is one), but by asking for this information from the receptionist, you gain an opportunity to establish a relationship with a key gatekeeper.

- **Dress the part.** Dress appropriately for the type of customer you are calling on, but, despite conventional wisdom, wearing a suit in today's business culture may not always be the best approach. In certain circumstances, wearing a suit screams "I'm a salesperson coming to get your money!" Sometimes a more stealthy approach works best. If you are calling on a young software development firm, Dockers and a collared shirt or even nice blue jeans might work best. If you are calling on an auto shop, you might want to wear clean work clothes. If you are calling on a bank or brokerage firm, a suit is appropriate. You can also adjust how you dress depending on who you are meeting in the company. If your first meeting is to accumulate intelligence to prepare for an eventual meeting with the decision maker (see above bullet), you might dress casually to talk with the receptionist, then wear a suit when you meet with the owner.

In Practice

Derek Robe provides marketing, sales, public relations, and writing services to small businesses in and around Kansas City, Missouri. He found success focusing on the often-overlooked small businesses in his area. As he describes it, "I provide marketing strategies tailor made for any small to medium-size business. I pick an infrequently canvassed, light industrial area and start walking into the businesses." Robe knew that many of these businesses have little or no marketing tools, frequently depending on word-of-mouth and repeat-customer business. "I walk up and start asking for the information that they give to their customers. Whenever I'm told they don't have any marketing materials, I know I'm at the site of an initially qualified lead."

Once he qualifies the prospect, Robe tries to meet with the decision maker. "Getting to the decision maker might take two or three visits. When I get the right person, and he or she asks me the 'What do you do?' question, I tell them 'we help businesses get more customers.' I ask for a time when I can come back for 20 or 30 minutes to hear his or her story and offer a few no-strings-attached suggestions. Then, I immediately offer to disappear! I get the appointment about one in ten times after talking to the decision maker."

Robe also found that, even if the business he was talking to was not interested in his services, the person was willing to provide him leads. "Usually, neighboring businesses are not in direct competition with each other. So owners and employees of one business will tell me about a neighboring business. Many times, I had the owner's name when I walked in, because I'd gotten the information in a previous cold call at a neighboring business."

46. Use a script for telephone cold calling

It's normal to be nervous when you're cold calling. However, it's not a good idea to talk off the top of your head when explaining your products or services. The person listening to you will allow you a very narrow time slot in which to keep his or her attention, so you must prepare yourself. The best way to prepare and keep from stumbling is to use a prewritten script.

Practice your script by reciting it into a recording device and playing it back. You can also practice your script on a cooperative friend or colleague.

Here are some additional tips for successful cold calling:

- **Narrow your pitch.** Cold calling works best if you can narrowly define your services. For example, a technical writer might do better at cold calling if he or she proposes specific paper and online help documentation rather than general "technical communication" services.

- **Set cold calling objectives.** Successful cold calling is a numbers game. You have to make many successful connections to produce new business. Set a specific day and time to cold call and the number of successful connections you will make. What is a "successful" connection? Consider a connection successful if you either talk directly to a decision maker or decision "influencer" or leave a message on the answering system. As you will learn later, leaving a message can serve as your verbal business card.

- **Define a successful outcome.** To make cold calling easier to handle, remember that you do not have to measure your outcome by how many prospects hire you on the spot. Instead, your goal should be to build a new relationship with someone who will want your product or service at some time. "Some time" may be today or a month from today. As such, there are three successful outcomes to your cold calling. The first and best outcome is scheduling a meeting with the prospect. Even if the prospect does not have a particular project in mind at this time, it's always a good idea to try and schedule a face-to-face meeting to describe your services and leave behind your marketing materials. If you can't schedule a meeting with the client, the second best outcome is a request for your marketing materials. The third best outcome occurs when the prospect admits that he or she cannot use your services, but refers you to other colleagues who can.

- **Pace yourself.** When you call a prospect, limit the small talk. Remember, you have a lot of calls to make and the time is precious. When you complete a call, keep going! Dial the next number without replacing the handset. If you put the phone down, you risk breaking your stride and becoming distracted by a less intimidating activity. You might want to consider purchasing a telephone headset. This will make the calls more comfortable and leaves both hands free to write or type notes.

Resources

Cold Calling for Cowards™

http://www.FootInTheDoor.com

Expert salesperson Jerry Hocutt conducts Cold Calling for Cowards™ seminars throughout the United States His seminar is specifically designed for cold calling on the telephone and calling on top-level decision makers. If you can't make it to the seminars, the website sells seminar audio tapes. The website includes sales tips and a free e-mail newsletter. For a fee, you can subscribe to the Keep in Touch customer contact program, which manages your contact list, sending e-mail postcards on a regular schedule to your business contacts.

47. Compile a good prospect list

As in mass mailing, you increase the potential success of your cold calling effort by using a targeted prospect list rather than a shotgun approach. One of the best ways to do this is to start your cold calling as a networking activity. Call your current clients and ask them whether they can give you the names of any colleagues who may need your services. This activity accomplishes three objectives. First, it builds your cold calling prospect list. Second, it provides an introduction to those prospects when you call them. Third, it helps maintain your relationship with your current clients. You may also uncover new opportunities with your current clients in the process. Here are some potential sources for a prospect list:

- Directories from professional organizations
- Industry advertisements
- Yellow Pages listings for your field
- Internet search engines
- Conventions/trade show mailing lists
- Industry publication mailing lists
- Business news stories.

48. Develop a script for voice mail

Before you start your cold calling campaign, you must prepare yourself for when you get bounced to the prospect's voice mail. When this happens, you can call again later without leaving a message or leave a sales pitch in your voice mail message. In many ways, if you are already nervous about doing cold calling, the prospect of leaving a voice message is even more anxiety ridden. A live listener will quickly forget your initial nervousness later in a conversation as you gain your footing and confidence, but if you try to leave a voice mail message unprepared, the answering system permanently records every self-conscious nuance of your pitch. Better to use a carefully crafted and practiced script for voice mail messages.

49. Delegate cold calling to a professional

If you're willing to spend some money and you don't want to do your own cold calling, why not delegate it? You can hire a telemarketing firm or public relations professional to promote your product or service. A good public relations person has developed a database of contacts that includes good working relationships with the media. Your PR person can write press releases, develop advertisements, get media stories about your company, place ads in magazines, and develop a marketing plan with you. Some even provide website hosting services. However, be prepared to pay for these services. Prices range from $300 to create a press release to $40,000 for a full-blown national media campaign.

Resources

Talion
> http://www.talion.com.
> Talion is a public relations firm that provides telemarketing services specifically designed for small companies. You can select from small, medium, large, or custom publicity campaigns for your product or service. The company can work with a list you provide or can provide a media list from its database. Programs start at about $450 per month.

Public Relations Society of America (PRSA)

http://www.prsa.org

33 Irving Place

New York, NY 10003-2376

(212) 460-1459

Contact PRSA to find a public relations professional for your business. The society provides a service called PR Power that can search its database for professionals with the public relations skills you require. Then they contact a number of candidates to determine their availability and present the resumes of several candidates. After you interview the candidates by telephone or in person, you select a qualified professional who meets your needs. In most cases, you complete the process in three days or less.

50. Delegate cold calling to a student intern

Another way you can delegate cold calling and save money is by tapping the student resources of your local universities. Check local colleges and universities that have business communications or marketing programs to determine whether they have internship programs. Find out the requirements for participating in the program. In most cases, a student will work with your company in exchange for college credits and working experience, but you may have to pay the school a stipend for administrative expenses. You may also decide to offer at least minimum wage to attract some of the brighter students. In return, you'll get the services of the student for a school semester, probably 10 to 15 weeks.

Although they probably will not have developed a set of media or industry contacts, student interns can cold call your list of prospects and send out press releases. You can also have them do research to add names to your prospect list by searching the Internet and reading business news stories in industry publications.

Resources

Internships

http://www.internships.com

This website lets you list your internship for entry in one of its printed national internship guides.

Encouraging Positive Word of Mouth

"In the new economy, consumers have built up antibodies that resist traditional marketing. That's why we need to stop marketing at people, and start creating an environment where consumers can market to one another."
—Seth Godin from *Fast Company* magazine issue 37 (August, 2000).

This quotation is from an article in which Seth Godin introduces the concept of the "ideavirus." The idea virus is an advanced technique based on an old concept—word of mouth. Positive word of mouth, reviews, and referrals are the best forms of marketing because a third party acts as your salesperson. You can harvest positive word of mouth from your customers, vendors, and even your "competition."

51. Request referrals from your clients

Whether it's a movie, song, book, website, programmer, or accountant, the most successful products and services get that way through word of mouth. Your clients probably operate in circles with other similar businesses that might be good prospects for your business. Here are some tips for asking for referrals:

- **Make sure you're asking a "happy" client.** Before you ask for referrals, there's a simple question you should be asking anyway. "Are you happy with my service?" You may think your clients are happy, but until you hear it from their mouths, you can't be sure. By asking this straightforward question, you can not only avoid the embarrassment of asking for

81

referrals from a secretly disgruntled client, but also do some damage control on your current work for the client.

- **Don't be afraid to ask.** Let your clients know you're always looking for new work. Don't let them assume you're booked up. If your work has satisfied a client's needs, you might be surprised how far they will go out of their way to help you. They may even refer prospects to you without asking, but it's possible they are so caught up with doing their jobs that they need a subtle prompt. It can't hurt to ask.

- **Don't restrict your request to professional contacts.** If you think the client would be receptive to it, you can ask the client to review his or her personal as well as professional contacts. Maybe the client knows someone on the bowling team who may be interested in your services.

- **Consider offering an incentive.** Offer a reward to anyone who refers work to you, but be careful how you administer it. If your client is a government entity, this might be considered a bribe. Even some large corporations may have restrictions on employees accepting incentives or rewards for referring work to vendors.

- **Make it easy for the client to make the referral.** If appropriate, provide extra business cards and brochures to clients so they can pass this information on to someone else.

- **Structure the information you want from the client.** If the client agrees, provide a form that steps the client through questions that help you collect targeted information intended to help you qualify the referral. A good way to do this is through a post-sale satisfaction survey.

Review your client list. While any satisfied client is a potential for referrals, start with the clients most likely to give you good referrals. Base your criteria on the following two factors:

1. **Does this client like me?** As mentioned above, make sure the client you are approaching is happy with your service or product and you have an excellent working relationship.

2. **How connected is the client?** Is the client active in professional organizations, trade associations, the local chamber of commerce? If the client has a high profile in the industry, he or she probably has many contacts.

52. Offer an incentive for referrals

As stated above, referrals are the best way for a business, particularly a service business such as consulting, to add new clients. Clients often provide referrals without expecting anything in return, but why not keep them interested by sweetening the pot with an incentive? When planning the rules for rewarding client referrals, you have to determine whether you will award the incentive for providing the contact information for the referral or only if and when the referral becomes a paying client.

Here are some ideas for rewarding your clients for referrals:

- **Free products or services.** If you operate a product-based business, offer some free product to the referring client if you gain a new client from the referral. If you operate a fee-based service business, provide a discount on any new business with the referring client for any referral that becomes a new client or offer free hours of service.

- **Cash.** Cash rewards are universally accepted. You can offer a flat amount when the referral becomes a client or base the reward on a percentage of the new account sale.

- **Gift certificates.** You can offer gift certificates that the client can apply to future transactions with your business. If gift certificates from your own business aren't appropriate, many businesses offer gift certificates for general products that your client might like. You can even purchase electronic gift certificates for online stores such as Amazon.com. Better yet, maybe you can combine advertising with another business issuing the gift certificate.

- **Magazine subscriptions.** A referring client may appreciate getting a paid subscription to an industry magazine or newsletter.

- **Gift baskets.** Perhaps you can create a gift basket containing candy, gourmet food, fun items, or a combination of the incentives mentioned above. If you don't want to put together the gift basket yourself, some gift-basket providers will customize one for you.

Resources

Gifttubes.com

http://www.gifttubes.com

This site provides a directory of corporate gift-basket providers through-out the United States. The gift designers listed in the directory offer predesigned gift baskets or can custom design one for your business.

Amazon

http://www.amazon.com

Amazon specifically designed a part of its gift certificate program for corporate gifts. Go to amazon.com and search for "gift certificates" to see what is offered. There are several corporate purchase and delivery options including e-mail and paper delivery. The e-mail version arrives within hours, and the paper version arrives in 3–7 days. You can also send gift certificates to multiple addresses all at once. Amazon also offers advanced corporate gift certificate options, such as discounts and self-distribution of gift certificate codes.

53. Set up reciprocal referrals with your "competition"

In some fields, your "competition" can provide some of your best re-ferrals. This typically works best for service industries in which there are not enough practitioners and when you don't want to expand your business by hiring more staff. When you network at meetings of professional organiza-tions, listen for any colleagues who seem to have more work than they can handle. Inquire whether they would be willing to refer or even subcontract some of their overflow to you.

By the same token, when you get more work than you can handle, re-ciprocate by referring the lead to a colleague. To maintain your reputation with both the prospect and your colleague, make sure you refer good pros-pects only to high-quality professionals who can do as good (or better) a job than you.

54.   Refer vendors to your clients

At the dry cleaners, have you ever seen brochures or business cards on the counter for other businesses not related to dry cleaning? In addition to cross-business promotions with complementary businesses, why not refer your favorite vendors to clients?

Analyze the vendors with which you do business. Select those vendors you are particularly happy with and with whom you have an excellent relationship. Contact them and tell them you want to refer them to your clients and ask them if they can reciprocate. If they agree, ask for extra copies of their brochures and business cards, and send them some of yours.

55.   Generate a post-project satisfaction survey

To assist in gathering information about client satisfaction, use a satisfaction survey. Depending on the type of your business, you can send the survey to your customers via regular mail or e-mail or place blank forms at your point of sale. This is a good way to find out what your customers liked and what they wished you had done better. If the customer is satisfied, ask them whether you can use them as a reference. If they are not completely satisfied, try to find out exactly why. Access their complaint and decide how you can turn an unhappy customer into a fan. You can try to correct the problem by offering some free product or consulting hours, a discount on the final bill, or a complete re-do of the work.

Here's an example of a satisfaction survey:

TWrite, Inc.
Post-project Satisfaction Survey

Company: _____   **Date:** _____

1. **Are you satisfied with the services provided by TWrite for your project:**

   ❏ Yes   ❏ No

2. **If no, please explain below:**

   _____

   _____

   _____

   _____

3. **What did you like best about the services provided by TWrite?**

   _____

   _____

   _____

   _____

4. **If you have any suggestions for improvement, please specify below:**

   _____

   _____

   _____

   _____

5. **Can TWrite use you as a reference?**

   ❏ Yes   ❏ No

6. **Can you provide a quote that we can use in our marketing materials?**

   _____

   _____

   _____

   _____

   _____

7. **Would you recommend TWrite to a colleague?**

   ❏ Yes   ❏ No

8. **Are there any colleagues, friends, or other contacts you can refer to TWrite? If so, please list them below:**

Name	Phone Number/Email

   Thank you for completing our survey. We look forward to working with you again!

Gaining Publicity

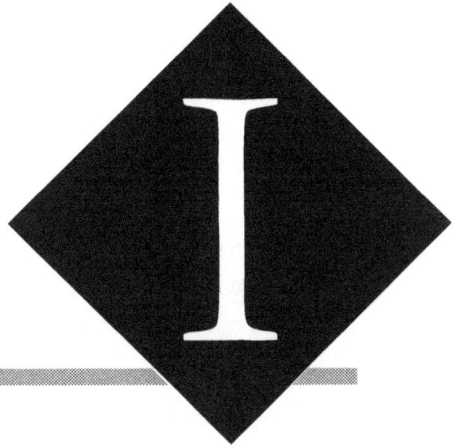

> *"All publicity is good, except an obituary notice."*
> —Brendan Behan (1923–64), Irish playwright. Quoted in: *Sunday Express* (London, 5 Jan. 1964).

Although large companies spend millions of dollars with public relations firms trying to get publicity for their business, free agents can accomplish a lot with less money and more sweat equity. Fortunately, getting publicity has less to do with spending money and more to do with your ability to tell a story that will drive consumers to a media outlet. If you're willing to do the work, a well written news release can generate interest from reporters and editors. If you can't get past the media gatekeepers for a full-blown news story, you can maintain a high profile in the media by writing letters to the editor, product reviews, and editorials.

56. Submit electronic news releases

There is nothing new about using news or press releases to generate a media story on your business. The newer twist on this venerable tool is electronic distribution. Rather than stuff hundreds of envelopes and incur mailing costs, you can distribute news releases to hundreds of media professionals using e-mail and the Internet. Electronic distribution is not only quicker and less expensive than paper news releases, but also provides a more usable version of your news release because an interested reporter can cut and paste the text without retyping. Because of the labor-saving advantages of electronic news releases, many media professionals prefer them.

You can accumulate your own database of reporters and editors or use an electronic distribution service such as Business Wire or PR Newswire. The advantage of a distribution service is that it keeps the list of media professionals up-to-date. These services also provide a platform to distribute multimedia news releases and webcasts.

Writing a good news release is an art in itself. There are entire books dedicated to the subject and the public relations professionals who specialize in effective news releases, so a detailed description of how to write an effective news release is beyond the scope of this book. However, here are some basic tips on increasing the odds of getting your news release noticed:

- **Make sure it's news.** If you want a media professional to take interest in your story, it has to be newsworthy. Typical business news releases include information about openings, expansions, moves, awards, company milestones, management hires, and financial reports. But as a small or one-person business, how many of these items will be of interest to a media professional? It's better if you can describe a related problem and a solution or provide some valuable content such as ten "how-to" tips.

- **Write efficient copy.** Harried editors often paste text from a news release directly into the published story without editing. Thus they may cut paragraphs without rewriting, and they tend to cut from the bottom up. So follow basic journalistic style. Make sure you have the five "W's"—who, what, when, where, and why—in the first few paragraphs. Analyze your copy to see how it will stand up if someone cut the bottom paragraphs.

- **Write a catchy headline.** To get editors to read your story, you have to grab their attention with the headline. When listed in an e-mail in box or on a news wire website, the headline is the only part of the release that is up front. So you have to make the most of this chance to get the editor to open the release and read it. Don't resort to loud tactics such as multiple asterisks, dollar signs, or exclamation points. Write the headline last, when you have a full picture of everything included in the release. For inspiration, visit the Business Wire (www.businesswire.com) or PR Newswire (www.PRnewswire.com) to see which headlines attract your attention.

Resources

PR Newswire

http://www.PRnewswire.com
Established in 1954, PR Newswire has offices in 14 countries and regularly transmits its clients news to outlets in 135 countries in 27 languages.

Business Wire

http://www.businesswire.com
Business Wire electronically transmits full-text news announcements from its clients to news media, financial markets, disclosure systems, investors, information websites, databases, and other audiences. By using Business Wire to distribute your news releases, you can specify the geographic markets, industry audiences, and editorial desks most appropriate for your announcements.

Shameless Marketing for Brazen Hussies: 307 Awesome Money-Making Strategies for Savvy Entrepreneurs

by Marilyn Ross and Curtis Killorn (Illustrator).
Buena Vista, CO: Communication Creativity; 2000, ISBN 0918880440.
Despite its title, this book is not for women business owners only. There is a wealth of information and resources for any small business including numerous ideas on getting publicity for your business.

57. Prepare product reviews

One way to get publicity for your business and establish yourself as an expert is to review products used by your customers. There are many outlets for published reviews, both in print and on the Internet. Trade magazines often solicit experts to regularly review relevant products and services. If you do a print review, the editor will most likely include a short bio of you at the end of the article where you can mention your business and what you do. You may be paid for the article, but even if you do it for free, the article has publicity value.

Online vendors such as Amazon.com also allow people to submit feedback and reviews of products they sell. Many of them also have a rating system for readers to rate the review. As you do more reviews and get more positive ratings, the site will typically highlight you as an expert reviewer by putting a small logo by your name. Most allow you to provide your e-mail address so someone can contact you about your review. When you submit a review of a product on these sites, you can embed information about you and your business in your "handle." A handle is a short description that the website allows you to use to identify yourself. For example, when you create a profile on Amazon.com, you could put your name, "John Smith," but there is enough space to include more information. Why not put "John Smith, President, ABC Consulting, Inc."?

You can also embed information about your business in the review itself, such as "When I used this product for my computer consulting business, I was amazed at how well it worked." However, be careful not to turn the review into a commercial for your business. Not only will the site administrator probably pull the review, but even if it gets through, readers will see it for what it is—an advertisement. If you confine your reviews to products you actually use and care about, your review will be more authentic.

You also have to decide whether you will do only positive reviews or both positive and negative reviews. The disadvantage of doing negative reviews is that even if readers agree with your assessment, a negative review is a downer and you risk alienating the product vendor. However, some readers may thank you for helping them to save money and time that would otherwise be wasted on a dog product.

Resources

epinions.com
http://www.epinions.com
Want to make money doing online reviews? This site does nothing but reviews of just about everything and pays a small fee when a browser stops to read a review. However, the payment is only a few cents per view. But who knows? If you become a popular reviewer, these few cents can add up.

Amazon.com
http://www.amazon.com
You can register with Amazon as a reviewer and write reviews about any of the products they sell. When you register, they provide space for you to type your bio. You can even provide a link to a photograph that you

have stored elsewhere on the Web. People who read Amazon reviews rate can vote on how they liked the review and if you get enough positive votes to land in the top 500 reviewers spot, they display a special logo next to any reviews you write.

Barnes & Noble

http://www.bn.com

Barnes & Noble have a more informal review system. You can write a review for any of their products right on the spot, without "registering" with them, by clicking on a link while viewing the product's web page. The link takes you to a form where you provide a star rating, headline for the review, the review text, your e-mail address, your name, and a brief statement about who you are. You can opt not to display your e-mail address.

58. Write an editorial

Another way you can use your writing skills to gain more publicity for your business is to write an editorial for your local newspaper or trade publication. Even if you don't want to write a full-blown editorial, you can utilize the "letters to the editor" section of a publication to submit an opinion about a subject relevant to your community or to your industry. Check your local papers and industry publications. Get the name of the editor and send in your editorial.

59. Become a quoted expert

Reporters are always looking for quotable sources for their stories. If you establish a reputation with the media as an expert, they will call on you for interviews. There are several ways you can establish your expert status. Here are some ways to get noticed by the media as an expert:

- **Write articles.** By providing "how-to" articles to industry publications, you help establish your expert status. These articles also give you a handful of clippings to send to the media.
- **Write a nonfiction book.** As a published author, you gain credibility on the subject of your book.

- **Register as a speaker.** As a registered speaker, you can not only gain additional income but also use the publicity about any speaking engagements as a platform for your expert status.

- **Become a spokesperson for your professional organization.** When the media needs statistics or other information related to your industry or profession, they will quote you as the spokesperson.

- **Register with "expert" directories.** There are several expert databases that the media consults when they need an expert for an article. Usually you have to pay a fee to be listed, but it may be worth it.

In Practice

Jim Salmons and Timlynn Babitsky think of themselves as "vision-driven opportunists" and "entrepreneurial free agents." They're founders of SohoDojo (SohoDojo.com), a nonprofit, independent, applied research and development laboratory supporting entrepreneurial free agents. They also invented the term nanocorp. They describe a nanocorp as "a ruthlessly small business." They explain, "By 'ruthlessly small,' we mean we are committed to a 'no growth' policy. Well, not entirely true. We mean no accretive growth; no getting bigger by adding more bodies to handle the workload."

The term nanocorp might have lapsed into obscurity if it weren't for Salmons' and Babitsky's persistence. After writer Dan Pink published an article in *Fast Company* magazine about free agent entrepreneurs, they made sure Pink knew about their work. "We approached him with persistent, provocative e-mails that somehow stayed just this side of driving him nuts." As a result, when Pink was writing his best-selling book *Free Agent Nation*, he interviewed Salmons and Babitsky and credited them with the nanocorp term in his book.

Salmons and Babitsky continue to use this technique to promote their work. As they describe it, "We've succeeded in a number of similar ways since then and we are getting better at this kind of promotion all the time."

Resources

Toastmaster International

http://www.toastmasters.org

Toastmasters is a nonprofit organization established in 1924. It promotes speaking to groups and working with others in a supportive environment. You can join a club in your area and make presentations at meetings. A typical Toastmasters club comprises 20 to 30 people who meet once a week for about an hour. The website publishes tips on giving speeches and presentations.

National Speakers Association

http://www.nsaspeaker.org

Established in 1973, the National Speakers Association (NSA) is the leading organization for experts who speak professionally. The association provides resources and education to advance the skills, integrity, and value of its members and the speaking profession. To qualify for membership, you must have received payment for at least 20 presentations; given 20 presentations to audiences of 15 or more as part of a salaried position; or earned at least $25,000 giving presentations within the last 12 months.

Authors and Experts

http://www.authorsandexperts.com

This site provides a searchable directory listing for the media and access to media want ads. The charge is $99 annually to be listed in the directory.

Radio-TV Interview Report

http://www.rtir.com

This trade publication has a circulation of more than 4,000 radio and TV producers in the United States and Canada. The magazine is published three times each month. Each issue lists 100–150 authors and other spokespeople available for live and in-studio interviews. You can pay for an ad that includes a contact person and phone number so interested radio and TV producers can get in touch to arrange interviews.

60. Conduct a survey

One way to gain publicity for your business is to conduct an industry survey—of your customers, vendors, or fellow professionals. The information could help you target the market for your services and products, and you can publicize the survey findings with a press release. If the survey is newsworthy, it might be reported in the newspaper, on radio, or on TV. If you don't want to do it alone, you can conduct a joint survey with the appropriate professional organization or other interested parties (i.e., your vendors or fellow professionals).

You can conduct a telephone survey, a mailed paper survey, or a self-directed online survey. If you're not sure how to conduct a good survey, you can employ the resources of a marketing house or survey service.

Resources

Ioxphere
http://www.ioxphere.com
This website conducts online surveys for a fee.

How to Conduct Surveys: A Step by Step Guide
by Arlene Fink and Jacqueline B. Kosecoff. Thousand Oaks: Sage Publications, 2nd ed., 1998, ISBN 0761914099
This is the second edition of this book. It provides step-by-step advice on preparing and evaluating surveys including computer-assisted and interactive surveys. The book also provides guidelines for preparing informed consent statements and ways to ensure a large enough sample to detect a difference between groups (if one exists).

Mail and Internet Surveys: The Tailored Design Method
by Don A. Dillman. New York: John Wiley & Sons, 2nd ed., 1999, ISBN 0471323543
This book, in its second edition, provides a guide for those who need to plan and conduct effective surveys. It covers maximizing response rates and getting feedback from self-administered, electronic, and mail surveys.

61.   Host a radio show

Depending on the size and format of your local talk-radio station, it's possible you could pitch the station's management on hosting a radio show. Make sure your subject is generic enough to appeal to a wide segment of the station's audience. Possible show ideas are starting a business, using your computer, investing, or purchasing real estate. Of course, it helps if you are a good speaker and can establish yourself as an expert on the subject. Also, it's easier to get the radio station's attention if you can line up some sponsors who are willing to purchase advertising time on your show.

Still can't interest a radio station in your idea? As strange as it sounds, some radio stations will sell a 30-minute or 1-hour segment of time to the public. The cost depends on the time slot, but most people who purchase time use it for an infomercial.

You can also try Internet radio. Hundreds of new radio stations are being added every year, and they're all looking for content. Similar to broadcast radio stations, Internet radio stations seek two things for a new show: First, they seek someone who is connected to an online community. If you publish an e-newsletter, host an e-mail discussion group, or manage a message board for a particular community, you might be a good candidate for an Internet talk radio show. Second, they look for a community that has a recognizable market for products. This is how they attract advertising to pay for the show.

Resources

wsradio.com
http://www.wsradio.com
This group produces Internet talk radio programs including many business programs. You can propose your own show idea by contacting Lee Mirabal, Vice President of Programming, at leemirabal@wsradio.com or 858-623-0199 ext 101.

Syndication.net
http://www.syndication.net
Created by syndication consultant Chris Witting, this site provides information about syndicating yourself. The site includes advice on getting syndicated, audio seminars on the subject, a syndication database, and industry news.

62.   Host a TV show

As part of their requirements for licensing, cable companies must set aside certain channels and provide equipment and studios to the community, so local individuals can develop noncommercial programs. These programs discuss community issues, promote educational and economic resources, and celebrate local talent and initiatives. It's called public access TV. Public access stations are operated primarily by community volunteers; they produce the shows and even work the cameras.

You can pitch your local public access station on producing your own cable show. The show should provide an educational benefit to the station's (and the community's) viewers. This will benefit your business because you establish yourself as an authority on the subject within the viewing range of the station. Don't know how to produce a TV show? Fortunately, the public access stations provide free or inexpensive training in video production and camera operation.

In Practice

Cable access is one path to getting on TV, but don't assume you don't have a shot at getting on your local broadcast channel. This is what Lee Welles, owner of MARS Fitness Services discovered. Each week she is the featured fitness expert on the Corning, New York, NBC Affiliate, WETM. How did she get this fantastic opportunity? By speaking up at the right time.

As she explains it, "I tagged along when my sister, who was a free-lancer for a company that produced commercials, delivered a tape to a new station manager. He mentioned starting up a new morning program. I said, 'You need a fitness expert, like myself, to come in and give your viewers tips each week.'" The station manager liked her idea and gave her a weekly, 3-minute segment.

The exposure provided an exceptional boost to Welles's business, which includes lectures and workshops on fitness for companies like Corning Incorporated. "I have been doing this five years and I am recognized wherever I go. The papers routinely call me for my advice. The public relations and positioning as 'expert' is amazing! I find the television experience gives me instant credibility wherever I present."

Resources

dmoz.org

http://www.dmoz.org/Arts/Television/Cable_Television
/Public_Access
Dmoz manages the Open Directory Project, the largest, most comprehensive human-edited directory of the Web. It is constructed and
maintained by a vast, global community of volunteer editors. Included in
the directory is a listing of several hundred public access stations.

63. Place your product on a game show

Where do you think they get the prizes for shows like Wheel of Fortune?
Ever notice how much time they spend describing a prize that a contestant
wins? This is because the prizes are "donated" by the companies that make
them—they pay a fee to place their product on these shows. Moreover, most
shows allow the company to include an 800 number and any "live action"
demonstration videos of the product or service. Be prepared for the cost. It
can be from $295 to $10,000. However, compared to the cost of a paid
commercial on the same show, donating a product can be a bargain, provided TV is the right medium for selling your product.

Resources

Game-Show Placements, Ltd.

http://www.gspltd.com/gameshow.html
For a fee, this company will place your retail product and selling message
in front of millions of viewers on national TV. If your retail product
costs $300 or more, it can be featured in promotional spots on popular
game shows for only $195 per spot. For retail products costing less than
$100, the spot fees range from $295 to $9,000.

64. Record an "interview"

You don't have to have a real radio or cable show to be the subject of an
interview. Find a tape recorder, a quiet room, and a friend with a good voice.
Write up a set of questions for your "interviewer" that will bring out the high

points of your business. One approach would be to create a "case study" about a client problem that you helped them solve.

After you create your "script," conduct a five-minute interview. Of course, this takes the form of an infomercial, but it acts as an audio brochure for your business. Once your recording is made, you could digitize it on your computer using your sound card. After you convert your interview to a digital format you can upload it to your website or put it on a CD-R along with samples and slide presentations.

Resources

Words on Tape: How to Create Profitable Spoken Word Audio on Cassettes and CDs

by Judy Byers. Audio Cassette Producers; 1st ed., 1997.
ISBN: 0965572145

This book provides a basic road map to create an audio product. It covers creating the script, recording, editing, mastering the tapes, duplication, and packaging.

Producing and Selling Your Own Audio Cassette (Single Tape Speaking Series)

by Gordon Burgett. Communication Unlimited, 2nd ed., 1996,
ISBN 0910167125.

This audio cassette steps you through the production of an audio cassette, including production and sales. It also covers royalties, copyright, piracy, dub masters, and much more.

65. Distribute reprints

Have you ever walked into a restaurant and seen a newspaper story with a positive review of the restaurant hanging on the wall? If your publicity efforts bear fruit in the form of a print news story, consider purchasing reprints from the newspaper or magazine that published the story. You could try photocopying the article, but a printed reprint is easier to read and includes any colors that appeared in the original publication.

In addition to framing and displaying a reprint in a public place, you can send reprints to your customers, put them in press or sales kits, and make them available at presentations.

Using Direct Marketing

"*I have discovered the most exciting, the most arduous literary form of all, the most difficult to master, the most pregnant in curious possibilities. I mean the advertisement. ... It is far easier to write ten passably effective Sonnets, good enough to take in the not too inquiring critic, than one effective advertisement that will take in a few thousand of the uncritical buying public.*"
—Aldous Huxley (1894–1963), British author. *On the Margin*, "Advertisement" (1923).

We've all received it. Some people call it "junk mail." But when it comes from you, it isn't junk, right? The old paradigm of direct marketing was to use direct mail to shotgun as many sales pieces as possible and hope for a 2% response. Today, because of overuse and shorter attention spans, this tactic is progressively less effective even for large organizations. Moreover, the cost of a large, mass-market mailing is far beyond the reach of most free agents.

Today, you have the choice of e-mail direct marketing as well as snail mail. At first glance, e-mail appears like the perfect direct-mail medium—it's a way to send a marketing piece, as many times as you want, basically for free. However, in the last few years spamming has created the same overuse problems that afflicts paper direct marketing.

So how should you approach direct marketing? Seth Godin, author of *Permission Marketing: Turning Strangers into Friends, and Friends into Customers*, believes that the answer lies in persuading consumers to volunteer attention.

In other words to "raise their hands." Godin does this by using games and contests to get people interested. You can also do this by using opt-in lists or by harvesting lists of contacts where you've already established a relationship.

66. Write effective copy

As marketing expert Godin says, "If you get permission to talk to customers, you'd better have something to say." Writing a good direct mail piece is an art unto itself. There are many good books and seminars on the subject. One way to learn how to write good direct marketing copy is to study effective pieces you have received in the mail. Covering all the rules are beyond the scope of this book, but here are a few basic tips:

- **Try to make your pitch a form of education.** Some marketers make their pitch letter look more like a newsletter than a sales letter. Include tips, resources, and other useful content that may not only make the recipient read the text but also retain it as a reference.

- **Draw readers in with a great headline.** Try using a question or emphasizing a benefit.

- **Focus on benefits.** Emphasize how you will solve your prospect's problems.

- **More is better.** Many veteran marketers believe that four to eight pages of content is optimal. In this instance, e-mail has an advantage because there is no extra weight and therefore no extra charge for additional content.

- **Provide contact information everywhere.** If readers want to act without reading the rest of the message, don't make them search for your phone number or e-mail. Include it at the bottom of the page, insert a link, or repeat this information in the message itself.

- **Use a P.S.** A postscript always stands out in a message. It's your last shot at getting the reader to act. Try using the P.S. to throw in something extra, such as, "If you call today, I'll provide your first consultation free of charge."

- **Include testimonials.** Include recommendations, testimonials, reviews, and the like to reinforce your value.

- **Include a call to action.** Usually in the last paragraph, ask the reader to act. Include a deadline as an incentive to act quickly.

- **If you need it, get help.** If you're not sure you can write an effective message for your campaign, consider hiring a marketing writer.

Resources

Permission Marketing: Turning Strangers Into Friends, and Friends into Customers

by Seth Godin and Don Pepper. Simon & Schuster, 1st ed., 1999, ISBN 0684856360.

Seth Godin is one of the world's foremost experts in marketing and online promotion. In this book, he proposes that you first need to get a buyer's permission with some kind of bait–a big discount, a free sample, a contest, a game or even just an opinion survey. After you get customer "volunteers," it's easier to establish long term relationships and get more of your customer's attention.

Permission-Based E-Mail Marketing That Works!

by Kim Macpherson. Dearborn Trade Publishing, 2001, ISBN 0793142954.

This book provides advice for someone just learning about permission e-mail marketing. It provides case histories with good and bad examples of e-mail marketing and helps you estimate your ROI for an e-mail campaign.

67. Develop a mail list from your own files

You can purchase a mail list or you can develop your own. You probably have a wealth of prospect information in your own file cabinet! Scour your files to find contacts that you can add to your mail list.

Some potential sources for mail list contacts are as follows:

* Previous and current clients
* Business cards you've collected
* Organizational directories
* Alumni directories
* Requests for information.

68. Procure direct-mail lists online

Like many other things, the Internet made the purchase of direct-mail lists easier. You can purchase lists with full addresses for a paper direct-mail campaign or lists with e-mail addresses for an e-mail campaign. List providers help you customize the list by selecting demographic information about your target audience including type (consumer or business), location, and type of business. Some providers allow you to purchase very small lists of 10 or 20 contacts.

When you consider purchasing a list, find out all you can about how the list provider maintains it. Find out whether it's an opt-in list, where the names came from, how current they are, how names are removed from the list, and what type of guarantee they come with. Some direct marketing experts suggest that you split the list so you can test two different versions of your message.

Resources

The following websites provide direct mail lists:

Words in a Row
http://www.wordsinarow.com/e-mail_lists.html

E-mail Results
http://www.e-mailresults.com/e-maillists.html

ZairMail
http://www.Zairmail.com

bCentral
http://www.bCentral.com

69. Market with postcards

With postal rates constantly increasing, postcards are your best value. There are four advantages to postcards: First, they are relatively inexpensive. Second, because of their size you are forced to create a short, concise message that may have a better chance of getting attention than a long letter. Third, you don't have to depend on the recipient's interest and initiative to open anything; your message is immediately in front of the prospect. Fourth, a postcard may pass through the hands of many people at the recipient address or sit out in the open as it makes its way through the internal mail distribution system of a company. This exposes your message to additional potential customers.

If you don't want to do the mail merge and mailing of postcards yourself, service providers are available. You can upload your mailing list, or in some cases you can purchase a mailing list from the provider. Providers have templates in the two basic sizes for postcards: 4 x 6 in. and 6 x 9 in. Providers offer the option of one-color or multi-color. You can use their pre-designed generic picture for the front or upload your own. Once you upload your information, they handle the merge and mailing.

With the money you save, consider using four-color postcards. To get around the limited footprint available for your message, consider sending a series of postcards, each adding new information.

Resources

VistaPrint

http://www.VistaPrint.com

If you want to get postcards printed, but mail them yourself, VistaPrint can print the job with standard 4 x 6 in. or larger 8.5 x 5.5 in. postcards. VistaPrint can also print other business materials such as business cards, stationery, labels, and brochures.

ZairMail

http://www.Zairmail.com

ZairMail provides complete direct mail services. You can submit your postcard design, text, and mailing list, and ZairMail will print and mail the postcards. If you don't have a mailing list of your own, the company has lists you can buy. It also handles standard letters and self-mailers.

Postcard Marketing Secrets

http://www.postcardmarketingsecrets.com

In addition to purchasing a copy of the electronic document Postcard Marketing Secrets, you can sign up for a free e-mail newsletter to get tips on marketing with postcards.

70. Add something bulky to your envelopes

Want to pique someone's curiosity and increase the chance that a recipient will open your sales letter? Place some type of bulky memento into the envelope; this could be a baby shoe, pen, letter opener, or screwdriver with your company logo. A word of caution is necessary here: It used to be a common sales tip to hand-address sales letters to important decision makers in an effort to increase the likelihood that they would open a personally addressed piece of mail. However, since the September 11 attacks and the anthrax incidents that followed, company mailrooms have become very watchful for "suspicious" packages, particularly bulky, hand addressed packages with no return address. Therefore, unless you know the recipient well, you should type or print the address of your correspondence and you should always include a return address.

Resources

These companies can produce small items with your company logo:

Nebs
> 500 Main Street
> Grouton, MA 01471
> 800-225-6380
> Fax: 800-234-4324
> http://www.nebs.com

Amsterdam Printing and Litho
> P.O. Box 701
> Amsterdam, NY 12010
> 800-833-6231
> Fax: 800-833-6231

71. Conduct a co-op mailing

Direct marketing can be expensive. You can cut the cost by getting together with complementary businesses, clients, or even other professionals in your field to conduct joint campaigns. For example, if you are a graphic artist, you could place a joint direct-mail campaign with a printer. If you had a successful project with a client helping them to bring a new product to market, you could pitch them on conducting a joint direct-mail campaign—they would have exposure for their product and you could demonstrate a client success story.

Raising Your Profile While Doing Good

"If you will think about what you ought to do for other people, your character will take care of itself. Character is a by-product, and any man who devotes himself to its cultivation in his own case will become a selfish prig."
—Woodrow Wilson (1856–1924), U.S. Democratic politician, president. Speech, 24 Oct. 1914, Pittsburgh, Pa.

The side benefit of volunteer work and supporting nonprofits and charities is that this work helps you maintain a high profile and come in contact with potential customers. However, in deciding to be a business philanthropist your priority should be to choose an organization that does work you believe in rather than one that will provide the best connections. If you volunteer for a professional organization, be certain you have the time to really help the organization. Given this premise, there are many ways you can combine your desire to help with some networking through volunteering or advertising through sponsorship opportunities.

72. Sponsor public radio

Many local public radio stations encourage businesses to donate by offering certain benefits that can advertise a product or service. Donations vary from station to station (ranging from $75 to $1,000), and not all stations have special business support categories.

Benefits offered by a station may include the following:

* Mention of your business on the radio
* Invitation to special networking events
* Listing in the station's annual report
* Listing in a "small-business sponsor" directory distributed to members and other businesses.

Resources

National Public Radio
http://www.npr.org
On the National Public Radio website, you can find a station near you by clicking on "find a station." See what your local station has to offer in the way of "business support."

73. Auction products or services for charity

Another way you can do good deeds and get some publicity for your business is to donate your products or services to a charity. Many charities conduct regular or silent auctions to raise money for their cause. By putting your offering on display, you bring attention to your business. Decide whether you want to focus on a local charity or an out-of-town charity. The advantage of focusing on a local charity is that it also provides an opportunity to network in your community. However, if remote delivery of your product or service is not too expensive, a charity auction located in another city can bring exposure to your business in a different market. Review the charities and nonprofit organizations you care about to find those that have auctions.

74. Perform pro bono work

You can directly support nonprofits and charities you care about by doing pro bono work. Pro bono means work provided without compensation for the public good. Although it's most common in the legal profession, any service business can offer to do what it does best for a nonprofit organization that it cares about. In addition to the opportunity to network in your community, performing pro bono work is particularly useful in building a portfolio of successful work if you are starting your business. There's nothing wrong with adding a description of the work you did for a nonprofit or charity to your promotional materials. It not only describes the work you do but also advertises the organization receiving the pro bono work.

75. Volunteer for a professional organization

One of the best ways to network in a professional organization of your peers is to volunteer to help run things. This gives you a high profile in the organization and potential access to the movers and shakers in your industry. The work you do in the organization can be a training ground for honing your project management and communication skills. By volunteering for the membership committee, you can build a better profile of the members in the organization. The highest profile work of a professional organization tends to be the newsletter and program committees. If you're willing to invest more time, you can volunteer to help or even chair these committees.

Resources

Association Central
http://www.associationcentral.com
To find a professional organization or association for your industry, Association Central provides a searchable database containing thousands of them.

Acquiring Listings

One of the best and least expensive forms of advertising is a listing in professional directories and resource guides. Sometimes you can acquire a listing by joining a particular professional or industry organization. In other cases, you have to attend a vendor certification program or go through a certification process to be listed as a certified provider.

76. Gain a listing in professional directories

Another side benefit of joining a professional organization is that your name is listed in the organization's directory. This listing is often your best advertising. Some organizations, particularly those made up of independent consultants, allow you to describe your business in their directory. Independent consultant organizations also actively distribute copies of their directory to potential industry clients. Try to include as much contact information as possible in your directory listing so potential clients have many ways to reach you. This information includes your address, phone and fax number, and e-mail and website addresses.

Some large organizations publish multiple directories for specific segments of their membership. They may have subgroups or special interest groups (SIGs) that publish their own specialized directories. If you are an active member of an organization that doesn't have a directory or you see a way to create a specialized separate directory, suggest that the organization management create one. Better yet, volunteer to coordinate creation of the directory with other interested members. It will require a commitment of time, but you might create an entirely new market for yourself and other members.

Resources

Directories of Trade and Professional Associations

Check out the Encyclopedia of Associations and/or the Directory of National Trade and Professional Associations of the United States (referenced in tip no. 34). These references can tell you which organizations in your industry publish directories.

77.   Gain a listing in resource guides

To be more valuable as references, many industry publications include special sections that categorize and list industry vendors. These publications may be industry magazines, computer newspapers distributed for free in major cities, or industry websites. Some provide a listing of website addresses, while others allow vendors to provide a paragraph describing their services. Often these publications offer this service to vendors without charge or as a free benefit of the subscription, while others charge a fee for a listing. Even if a widely distributed publication charges a fee for a listing in its resource guide, the fee is usually lower than that for a display ad in the same publication.

Survey your industry publications to find those that provide resource guides. Find out which ones include listings as part of the membership or subscription and which charge a fee for listing in their resource guide. Then target your subscription and advertising dollars accordingly.

Resources

Summit Consulting Group

http://www.summitconsulting.com

Master consultant and author Alan Weiss maintains this site. Weiss is author of *Million Dollar Consulting: The Professional's Guide to Growing a Practice, 3rd ed.* (McGraw-Hill, 2003) and many other books on consulting. In addition to a wealth of free information and articles available for consultants, Weiss maintains the Summit Resource List. He provides this list for free to those who are seeking subcontractors in consulting, speaking, training, facilitation, and similar business services. For a one-time maintenance fee of $50, you can add your name to the list. Weiss actively markets the list in his books, newsletters, and articles.

78. Become certified for a vendor's product

Many industry vendors provide a certification program for consultants who use their products. This practice is quite prevalent in the computer industry in which companies like Microsoft, Adobe, Novell, and Macromedia maintain industry recognized certification programs. There are two main benefits to certification. First, the certifying organization typically provides a logo that graduates of these programs can display on their business cards, stationary, and website. This logo provides verification of your credentials that your clients can easily recognize. Second, these programs may provide some form of referral system for graduates. The level of referral assistance varies; some vendors only list you in their directory of certified professionals, while others actively refer clients to you.

If you plan to become certified on a vendor product to increase your credentials, assess the vendor's referral program for certified professionals. Ask the vendor whether it provides its clients with a listing of certified professionals and whether it directly refers clients. You may decide that it's better to be certified by the number two vendor with an active referral program rather than the number one vendor that provides a listing to customers only on request. Of course, if you can afford it, you could complete both certification programs.

Resources

Microsoft Certifications

http://www.microsoft.com/traincert

This site describes all of Microsoft's certification programs.

GoCertify

http://www.gocertify.com

GoCertify is an online resource for certification information: certification descriptions, costs, requirements, perquisites, and contact information. Information is available on more than 500 certifications from more than 90 vendors.

Transcender

http://www.transcender.com

This site sells self-study and simulation software to prepare candidates for Microsoft certification exams.

CertiPort

http://www.certiport.com

Certiport, Inc. is the exclusive worldwide provider of the Microsoft Office User Specialist (MOUS) program. It also administers the more generic Computing Core Certification (IC³). The site includes a searchable database of certification centers (called "iQcenters") where you can find the nearest location where you can take the tests. The site also sells preparation CDs for the certifications it administers.

79. List your business in the yellow pages

Not every business can benefit from a yellow pages listing, but even a basic listing might be worth considering, especially because there are now online versions of the paper telephone directory. To place a yellow pages ad, you have to make many important decisions. First, there are more directories than there used to be. In addition to the telephone company servicing your area, many other telecommunications and publishing entities publish and distribute directories. This introduces some competition for ads, you have to decide which directory or directories have the best chance of finding a home with your client base.

Once you decide on the directories in which you want to list your business, you have to select an appropriate category or categories that your clients are most likely to look in when they need your services. You may want to be listed in more than one category, and often the second category is less expensive. Also, you need to decide whether you belong in the consumer yellow pages or the business-to-business version. As one veteran consultant points out, "In my experience, a yellow pages listing is expensive, but people use it. Don't count on the directory publisher to help you classify your listing. Think like your potential clients, then look through the yellow pages for the right category."

Maximizing Your Business Cards

"An identity would seem to be arrived at by the way in which the person faces and uses his experience."
—James Baldwin (1924–87), U.S. author. The Price of the Ticket, "No Name in the Street" (1985; first published 1972)

Business cards are your most important paper marketing tool. In addition to providing contact information, they are, in fact, a "small billboard" for your business. They are the easiest marketing device to carry and distribute, so take full advantage of this medium. With numerous vendors available to print your cards, it's inexpensive to include color and raised lettering. At least one vendor provides free business cards if you let them include their logo on the back.

Today's technology provides many variations on this old workhorse. With preprinted card stock you can create different, custom versions of your business card and easily change information with little waste. CD-R business cards provide a way to distribute entire presentations in the palm of your hand. This new medium extends the reach of the little 3½ x 2 in. marketing device that amplifies our identity.

80. Rethink your business card

Don't take your business card for granted. There are many ways to maximize your message while minimizing your costs. You can have a quick printer make the cards for you or print them yourself on a color ink-jet printer. The advantage of using a printer is that the card stock is sturdy, and you can add special features such as raised letters. The disadvantage is that if you have to change anything (your phone number, address, e-mail address), you will have to throw out all your old cards and go back to the printer for more.

At a minimum, your business card should include the following:

- Your name
- Company name
- Business phone number
- Cell phone number
- Business address
- E-mail address
- Fax number
- The URL for the company website.

In addition to all the information listed above, here are some tips for designing your business card:

- **Use a splash of color.** Design your card in an attractive color that fits your company image. However, don't use too many colors. You can have a graphic artist design a simple, one- or two-color logo or you can put your name or company name in a colored font.

- **Use both sides of the card.** Rather than trying to cram all your contact information on one side of your business card, keep the front attractively simple and use the back for detail information. If you need even more space, use a folded business card format.

- **Leave space for notes.** Leave space on the reverse side of your business card for you or the recipient to write notes. For example, if you attend a seminar and the speaker offers to send you additional information, you can write the specifics of your request on the other side of your business card. When the speaker goes through all the business cards collected at the event, your note will remind him or her what you're requesting.

- **Avoid conspicuous titles.** To make an impression or as a matter of pride, you may be tempted to include a title for yourself on your business card. You might want to avoid including a title such as president, CEO, or chairman on your business card. When you're a one-person business, clients may question the purpose of such a title. Actually, the only time you'll have to use a title is when you sign contracts, particularly if you are acting as an officer of your own corporation. If you think you must have a title on your business card, you could use owner, principal, or consultant.

- **Reprint rather than mark up.** If you have to make a change to the information on your card, have new ones printed as soon as possible. Avoid trying to salvage the incorrect cards and save money by scratching out the incorrect information and manually writing the new information. You can do this in a pinch if you are close to getting new cards, but hand-written corrections to one's own business card projects a poor image.

- **Put extra business cards where you need them.** Have you every rushed out of the house to go to a professional meeting or a social event and realized that you forgot your business cards? You can minimize the situations in which you are caught without extra business cards by staging stacks of business cards in places and with items you are most likely to have with you when you leave your house. Consider storing your cards in your wallet, car, briefcase, personal organizer, and backpack.

- **Laminate copies of your business card.** Someone should do a study to determine whether more business deals have been done in a Jacuzzi or around a swimming pool than on a golf course. When you attend water sports, you don't have to leave your paper business cards behind. Laminate some copies of your business cards and stuff them in your bathing suit.

Here's an example of a business card that uses both sides:

[FRONT]

[BACK]

Resources

VistaPrint

http://www.VistaPrint.com

If you agree to include the VistaPrint logo on the back of your business cards, the company will print 250 cards for free. VistaPrint will also print premium business cards without the logo. The free business cards give you 30 design choices, versus 300 for premium business cards. VistaPrint can also print other business materials such as postcards, stationery, labels, and brochures.

81.   Customize your business cards

With the ability to print your own business cards from your laser or ink jet printer, you can create custom targeted business cards. If your business services several different industries, you could create a customized card for each industry, emphasizing specific services or benefits for each type of customer. You could also create different business cards emphasizing specific services for your business. For example, if you are a graphic designer, you could have a card that emphasizes your general corporate design services and one that emphasizes your website design services.

82.   Carry blank business cards

How often have you encountered this situation? You meet a great new prospect at a networking function. You ask for her business card, but she admits she either forgot her cards, ran out of them, or is having new cards printed up. You could give her your card and hope she follows up with her contact information, but that puts the burden on her.

The answer is to carry blank business cards. You can get a sheet of blank business cards and break them apart without printing on them or you can print blank forms with lines for name, phone, address, e-mail, printed on the card.

83.   Use business card CD-Rs

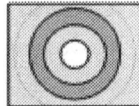

A new digital twist on the traditional business card is the business card CD-ROM. It works the same as a standard CD-R, but is cut to approximately the shape of a standard business card and has about 40 megabytes of storage capacity.

This new format is a great new and effective marketing tool because you can put things on the CD-R that you could never put on a standard paper business card. You can create a multimedia presentation or an interactive brochure, include samples of your work, or distribute software demos. If you want to burn your own business card CD-Rs, you need a standard CD burner. You can also purchase labels for your finished CD-Rs that you can print through your laser or ink-jet printer.

If you don't want to develop, burn, and label business card CD-Rs yourself, there are many development and duplication service firms available to help you. Some mainly provide duplication services and print a more professional label on your CD-Rs, while others also can develop an entire multimedia presentation for you.

Resources

Business-CD
http://www.business-cd.com
This company can help you custom design a digital business card with a multimedia presentation and burn it on a business card CD.

84. Save and organize business cards you receive

Collect business cards and save as many as you can. Collect them from people you meet at professional meetings, book clubs, reunions, school meetings, and other networking events. After a while, the business cards will start to pile up. How do you organize and keep track of the contact information on these cards? There are several options. You can physically organize business cards in a Rolodex or a binder that has plastic inserts with pockets for business cards.

If you have the discipline to do it, you can type the information from the business cards you collect into a contact management program such as Microsoft Outlook or ACT. If you want to save some time, you can use a scanner with text recognition software to electronically collect contact information from business cards.

Resources

CardScan Business card scanner
www.CardScan.com
This device is a small scanner optimized for scanning business cards. Several models are available that can scan in black and white and in color. Once scanned, the software uses text recognition technology to automatically enter the card's contact information in contact software such as ACT or Microsoft Outlook.

Using Paper Marketing Tools

Although technology has diverted many marketing efforts into a digital medium (e-mail, websites, banner ads, and so on), there are any number of ways to communicate your marketing message with good old-fashioned paper.

The standard materials are envelopes, brochures, and resumes. With some creativity, you can squeeze marketing value out of these workhorses. In addition, other paper materials that you regularly send out may not be obvious marketing vehicles, but can include or reinforce your marketing message. For example, have you considered what you can do with invoices and thank you cards?

85. Market with envelopes

Envelopes provide an opportunity to communicate something more than your return name and address. There are several ways you can spice up your envelopes to make them stand out, particularly when you are mailing marketing information and you want to increase the chances that the recipient will open the envelope. However, you don't want your envelopes to look like one from a sweepstakes promotion. To maintain your professional image, limit the amount of blatant advertising displayed on your envelope.

123

You could print a company tag line or communicate company news such as "Now available in your area!" You could also alert the recipient to a promotional discount such as "Free consultation! See inside for details."

You can print extra information on the front, back, or both sides of the envelope. If you print on the front, print your extra message on an angle. Most word processing packages provide some way to do this or you can have a commercial printer preprint your message. Or use clear labels to print your message and stick them on the envelopes.

Of course, you cannot obscure the recipient or return address information. One advantage of printing on the back of the envelope is that most people turn an envelope over when they start opening it. When they do, they see your message without any competition from the address information on the front.

86. Market with brochures

Many marketing experts are advising businesses to move away from the traditional brochure and toward media or information kits. The problem with brochures is that if they are professionally printed, you have to keep your information generic, which severely limits their value to a potential customer or client. The 200 brochures you had printed become obsolete over time and you have to toss your remaining stock.

However, properly designed, a brochure can have value as a marketing device. For example, if you attend a professional organization or a chamber of commerce meeting, you may be able to display your marketing materials on a table. In this case, a brochure may have a greater impact than a stack of business cards. Similarly, when you meet a prospect at a meeting, a brochure may stand out more than a business card (i.e. your business card might go unnoticed when the prospect dumps out a stack of them at home).

If you decide to use a brochure, here are some tips:

▪ **Print it yourself.** Rather than tie up your money by professionally printing your brochure, use pre-designed brochure stock that's available from many office supply stores or from Paper Direct. This has several advantages. First, you print only the number of brochures you need at any given time, saving waste. Second, you can adjust to changes in your business such as a new address or phone number. Finally, you can customize the brochure for specific industries or types of clients.

- **Create a job aid.** As an alternative to the traditional brochure touting your services and benefits, consider giving the brochure itself some value. Transform your brochure into a job aid. A job aid provides tips, information, or procedural shortcuts to complete a task. For example, if you are a website designer, you might provide a job aid that includes a list of HTML commands. An accountant might provide business owners with a calendar of key filing dates and descriptions of required forms. You can do this while mixing in information about your company. The goal is to create something that the recipient will keep. You can even laminate it into a sturdy reference. How about creating a bookmark?

- **Use plastic stand-up displays.** When you provide your brochures on a table at an event, use a plastic stand-up display to show the brochures. This gives the brochures a higher profile that can be seen from a distance. Plastic stand-up displays are inexpensive, so you can leave them at the event and use a new one at the next event.

Resources

Paper Direct

http://www.PaperDirect.com

Paper Direct provides cost-effective, professionally designed 3- and 4-panel preprinted brochures on which you can print your own information.

87. Create multiple versions of your resume

Most working people have a resume, but you might consider maintaining separate resumes for different purposes. Here are some examples:

- **Industry versions.** If your business services clients from different industries, consider having a different resume for each industry that your business targets. You can emphasize particular industry experience and other clients you've worked with in that industry.

- **Electronic versions.** If you are going to submit your resume to job sites or send your resume as an e-mail attachment, you should have an electronically friendly version of your resume. You should have one that is straight ASCII text (i.e., no formatting such as bold or italics) so that some-

What is it?

Adobe Acrobat is a software program that creates Portable Document Format (PDF) files. **PDF** is a file format that preserves all the fonts, formatting, graphics, and color of any source document, regardless of the application used to create it. Although you have to purchase the appropriate Adobe software to create PDF files, anyone can read your files on any type of computer with Acrobat reader software, which Adobe provides for free.

RTF stands for Rich Text Format. It is a Microsoft standard document format that most major word-processing programs can read and write. Unlike plain ASCII text, it allows the use of font styles and formatting. You might already have word-processing software that can output a document in RTF, so you don't have to purchase any additional software to create an RTF document.

one without the same word-processing software can read the resume. If you still want to be able to submit a resume that retains formatting, consider creating Adobe Acrobat and/or RTF versions.

- **Customized versions.** You may want to customize a resume for particular clients or companies where you can emphasize specific project or business experience.

88. Add a message to your invoice

One way to maintain a good relationship with clients is to add a message to invoices. It can be as simple as a brief message on the invoice itself or as elaborate as a newsletter enclosed with the invoice. The message could be entertaining, such as a different quotation from a famous person on each invoice or it could describe new services or products you're offering. If you come across a news story that you think your client might find interesting, include the clipping in the envelope with your invoice and a personal note. Most clients will appreciate that you took the time to pass the article on to them.

89. Use thank you cards

Everyone likes to get a "thank you." Your customers, clients, colleagues, and vendors are no different. Liberally send thank you cards to everyone who touches your business. In addition to thanking customers and clients for their patronage, use thank you cards to acknowledge colleagues who sent you work and vendors who went out of their way to get something done for you. When you send thank you cards, handwrite a short, personal note, and sign the card. People will remember you did this just as you would remember someone who acknowledges you.

To find blank thank you cards, visit Staples, Office Max, Office Depot, or any office supply store. You can also print your own custom thank you cards on ink jet card stock. Avery makes several types of blank card stock for ink-jet printers.

Resources

Avery

http://www.Avery.com
To find thank you cards, visit your local office supply store or Avery's website.

In Practice

Sending thank you cards is good. Sending thank you cards with a gift is even better. That's what Andrea Price, owner of Andrea Price Project Management & Implementation, discovered. As she explains, "It is common to send out cards when you have news to tell, but at times when I want to say 'thank you' to clients for a referral or drop them a line for no good reason, I slip in a Starbucks gift card." Price has found that this relatively inexpensive technique (she estimates she's spent about $75 on gift cards) gets more notice than other methods of direct mail. "When I send postcards to celebrate being in business for seven years, it requires little or no response. When I send a client a mocha chino latte, they usually write back to say 'thanks,' and that warms up the relationship."

Price also found that, although it doesn't have the same shelf life as a pen or mouse pad with a company logo, her thank you cards help build stronger relationships with her clients. "One client was so pleased with the gift that she called to tell me she wanted to use her Starbucks card to meet me for coffee so she could find out what I'm currently working on."

Using Signage

> *"Billboards, billboards, drink this, eat that, use all manner of things, everyone, the best, the cheapest, the purest and most satisfying of all their available counterparts. Red lights flicker on every horizon, airplanes beware; cars flash by, more lights. Workers repair the gas main. Signs, signs, lights, lights, streets, streets."*
>
> —Neal Cassady (1926–68), "Leaving LA by Train at Night, High ..." in The *First Third and Other Writings* (1971).

Just as e-mail and websites have not eliminated paper marketing tools, today's technology has not eliminated the value of good old-fashioned, sign-on-the-street marketing, especially when you use signage to leverage your digital marketing by advertising your website.

If your business is small and service oriented, you may assume that signage is irrelevant or too expensive. You may also assume that the sign may not get enough exposure to justify its use. However, the cost of simple signage that travels where you go is within reach of almost any small business, even the one-person kind. So get ready to hang out your shingle.

90. Attach a magnetic sign to your car

You see them on the road all the time: cars, trucks, and buses with advertising on the side or back panels. There's an easy way you can do this on your own vehicle without ruining it. If you use a sign shop to create a magnetic sign for your vehicle, you can advertise your business wherever you drive during the day and then remove the signs during the evening when you might not want to show up in your "ad car." In addition to a magnetic sign, these shops can create self-stick strips of plastic (for the inside of the back window) with information such as your website address.

Resources

Thrifty Signs
http://www.thriftysigns.com
In addition to regular magnetic signs, this company designs very inexpensive bumper magnetic signs appropriate for a URL address, phone number, or company name.

MagneticSigns.com
http://www.magneticsigns.com
This company offers free design and layout of your sign. Submit your request online by filling out a form.

91. Place a lawn sign in front of your house

You see them every election year: homes with in-ground political signs touting candidates for office. Painters and construction contractors also use them. What's good for politicians and painters is good for you. Depending on the type of business and the amount of traffic in your neighborhood, you may want to put a sign on your lawn advertising your business.

You probably should check with your local government to determine whether any restrictive ordinances apply. If there are no restrictions, you can have a sign made at a sign-making service or graphics house. What should you put on your sign? Keep the message short. At most, you probably should include your business name and phone number. For example "Joe Smith's Hardwood Floors 999-876-2234." A good candidate for your lawn sign is the address for your website.

Where should you put your lawn sign? If you're on a corner, that's a prime spot, the intersection of two streets. Otherwise, put it in the best place to be seen by motorists or foot traffic. If you operate a business that does work at the client site (like the previously mentioned painter or construction contractor), you may be able to display the sign there, if your customer approves. Make sure the sign is not obscured by foliage and it doesn't block any official municipal signage (stop signs, street names, and so on).

Resources

Thrifty Signs

http://www.thriftysigns.com
In addition to magnetic and bumper signs, this company provides lawn signs.

92. Create clothing with your business name

Well-known corporations do it, so why shouldn't you? As part of your branding strategy, you can have baseball caps, t-shirts, jackets, or tote bags printed with your name, logo, phone number, and website address. With some promotion printing companies, you can purchase items in quantities as low as 24 units.

There are many uses for these items. You can give them to customers who you've done work for or give them to prospects who visit your booth at a trade show. Give them to friends and relatives so they can proudly advertise your business as they go about town. Of course, you can advertise your business by wearing these items yourself. When you schedule a meeting with someone who doesn't know what you look like, you can identify yourself by wearing a piece of clothing with your company name on it.

Resources

These companies can create clothing with your business name:

Nebs

500 Main Street
Groton, MA 01471
800-225-6380
Fax 800-234-4324
http://www.nebs.com

WearGuard

141 Longwater Drive
Norwell, MA 02061
800-677-6060
http://www.WearGuard.com

Amsterdam Printing and Litho

P.O. Box 701
Amsterdam, NY 12010
800-833-6231
Fax 800-833-6231

CafePress.com

877-809-1659
http://www.cafepress.com
Ever wish you could open your own brand specific gift shop like Disney or Harley Davidson? CafePress.com provides an exciting option to create customized products and apparel with zero upfront costs. You can choose from over 50 items including T-shirts, jerseys, hoodies, ceramic and stainless steel mugs, lunch boxes, posters and framed prints, caps and visors, stickers, books, CDs, and bags.

They provide all the tools and services you need to design custom products and build an online shop without investing in any inventory or software. There are no setup, pre-printing, or inventory fees because they only imprint an item when it is ordered. Every time you sell an item, they keep the base price and pay you your markup cost. With this service, you can create a whole new business and revenue stream by putting your custom logo or image on common products.

Marketing With a Web Site

"It's given new meaning to me of the scientific term black hole."
—Don Logan, U.S. businessman, president and chief executive of Time Inc. Quoted in *New York Times*, (November 13, 1995), His response when asked how much his company had spent in the last year to develop Pathfinder, Time Inc.'s site on the World Wide Web.

The World Wide Web has become so ubiquitous in a relatively short time, it's hard to remember what we did without it. Having a website today has become as essential a marketing tool as having a telephone. For a free agent, a website can provide a relatively inexpensive way to distribute key information not only to prospects but also to current clients.

Perhaps the best use of a website for the small-business owner is as an interactive brochure. Imagine having the option of giving someone your business card with your website address rather than an expensively printed (and bulky) four-color paper brochure. Imagine offering capabilities beyond any paper brochure, such as downloading samples of your work or answering client questions up front. This is the power of the Internet.

However, once you've created a website, it doesn't automatically mean that the world will come to you any more than having a telephone means new customers will magically start calling you. Unlike mass marketing, your message is not broadcast on the Internet simply because you have a website. Instead, your website waits for someone to come knocking on your door. So creating a website is only part of the plan. Like your telephone number, you also have to let people know about your website address.

133

93. Create a website

Considering the potential of a website, there is no reason not to have one for your business. You can learn how to create the pages for your website yourself or hire a qualified professional to help you. Many programs for designing websites are available. Even the latest versions of the most popular word-processing software can convert your information into a Web-ready document. Many website providers also have pre-designed templates; you fill out a form and the system generates your website for you.

Resources

E-commerce web services

These sites provide e-commerce services for building an online storefront to sell products. They usually provide simple templates for filling in your company and product information:

bCentral
http://www.bcentral.com

eCongo
http://www.econgo.com

Yahoo! store
http://www.store.yahoo.com

Free Host Sites

Here is a list of several popular sites that will host your website for free:

Yahoo GeoCities
http://www.geocities.com

GeoCities offers 15 megabytes of storage space on a high-traffic site organized around a community theme. The free version of the service requires you to accept Yahoo ads on your website. If you want a more formal business presence on GeoCities and you are willing to pay a monthly fee, GeoCities offers a range of upgraded services for a modest monthly fee. Upgraded services include no Yahoo ads and more disk space.

Angelfire Communications

http://www.angelfire.com

Angelfire is part of the Lycos network. In exchange for allowing advertising, this Web hosting site offers several goodies such as 20 megabytes of free storage space, assistance creating a website, automated polls, and guest books. You can advertise your business on your page, run banner link exchange programs, create a guest book, choose from a variety of graphics, and add sound files. If you want to get rid of their ads and add more storage space, you can upgrade to Angelfire Plus.

Tripod

http://www.tripod.com

Tripod is also a part of the Lycos network and offers many of the same features as Angelfire.

Webspawner

http://www.Webspawner.com

Webspawner provides one free page of space. Although the free service is limited to one page, Webspawner has a simple setup process without HTML that requires you only to fill out an online form. Considering the limited size of the free area in Webspawner, you may want to consider setting up a more robust site on one of the other free host sites and use your Webspawner website to link to your main site.

94. Sell on auction sites

If you have a physical product that you can easily ship to customers anywhere in the world, consider selling your item on auction sites such as eBay. You can use this site to move some excess inventory or as a relatively inexpensive online store. Most major auction sites provide an option for merchants to set up shop on their sites to continuously sell regular inventories of products online. To make sure you can make a profit using auction sites, you can take advantage of the reserve feature that ensures your auction will not go through unless the bidding passes a certain minimum that you set. You can also sell at a fixed price or use the "buy it now" feature to sell to impulse buyers who don't want to compete in the bidding process.

Resources

eBay

http://www.ebay.com

With 42 million users, this is the most successful auction site. The company charges a small listing fee and another fee if your item is successfully sold. In addition to participating in auctions, regular merchants can set up an eBay Store, in which you sell your fixed-price and auction items from a special eBay page. You can create customized categories, include your own logo, and list store descriptions and policies. All your merchant listings contain an eBay Store icon and link that invites buyers to visit your eBay Store. eBay includes your store in the eBay Store Directory, which is designed to promote all stores. You also receive your own personalized eBay Store Web address.

There are three levels for eBay Stores, from $9.95 to $499.95 per month: basic, featured, and anchor. At the basic level you are listed in the eBay Stores Directory and in every Category Directory where your items are listed. eBay sorts stores based on item count within each category level. With the featured level, eBay rotates your store through a special featured section on the eBay Stores home page and gives you better placement in "Related Stores" search and listing pages, and on Category Directory pages. The anchor level showcases your logo in the eBay Stores Directory pages, provides premium placement in "Related Stores" search and listing pages, and guarantees you 1 million impressions of your logo throughout eBay.com.

uBid.com

http://www.ubid.com

uBid operates in a manner similar to eBay. A small listing fee is charged to place something on the auction site and another fee if an item is sold. In addition to regular auctions, there is the uBid Shop, a customizable online store with up to 11 unique departments, your own logo graphic, and 6 color options. There are also options for placing a rotating logo in the "Featured Shops" section of uBid Shops home and the category page on which your shop is listed.

Amazon Marketplace & zShops

http://www.amazon.com

Through Amazon Marketplace, you can sell individual quantities of your used or new items on the same page as Amazon.com sells the same item new. If you have a larger quantity of items to sell, you can open a zShop on Amazon. zShop sellers must register for the Pro Merchant Subscription. Amazon charges Pro Merchant Subscribers a monthly fee to maintain as many as 40,000 items. If your listings exceed 40,000 at any given time, there is a nominal listing fee for each additional individual listing. Amazon also provides Pro Merchants volume listing tools, fulfillment reports, and transaction reports.

Yahoo auctions

http://auctions.shopping.yahoo.com

On the Yahoo auction site where, there are regular auctions and a Yahoo Store for online merchants. Yahoo charges listing and successful sales fees in the same manner as the other auction sites; to open a Yahoo Store, they charge a monthly fee. The Yahoo Store fee includes credit card processing, although you have to sign up separately with their merchant account processing vendor and pay the transaction fees when someone purchases from your store with a credit card. Yahoo also has something called Bulk Loader, which saves time and effort by automating the process of submitting multiple auctions. With Bulk Loader, you can upload several items at once by creating a Comma Separated Values (CSV) file from a spreadsheet program like Microsoft Excel. With another tool called Seller's Manager, you don't have to be online to create and manage Yahoo auctions. Seller's Manager tracks and manages Yahoo auctions offline, from your computer and, similar to Bulk Loader, saves you time by streamlining the process of adding auctions.

Andale

http://www.andale.com

Andale is an online auction automation service that helps manage all aspects of the auction process. The service integrates with major auction sites such as eBay, Amazon, and Yahoo to give you a single place to manage all your online sales activities. Andale offers such services as sales research, image hosting, counters, feedback management, and sales reports. In addition to selling items on the auction sites, you can create your own online store on the Andale site. The research feature is particularly useful, and currently, it's free. If you enter the type of item you are planning to sell, Andale checks recent listings of the same item on the auction sites it monitors and gives you a report detailing the average final bidding price, the categories used, and a wealth of other information.

AuctionWatch

http://www.auctionwatch.com

AuctionWatch offers downloadable Windows-based applications that help you manage sales on the major auction sites directly from your desktop. Among the services offered are image hosting, inventory management and listing creation, merchandising and listing, direct marketing and promotion, automated checkout, automated tracking, and order fulfillment. In addition to selling items on the auction sites, you can create your own online store on the AuctionWatch site. A new feature assists you with processing nonpaying eBay bidders by submitting both eBay alerts and credit requests on your behalf.

AuctionWorks

http://www.auctionworks.com

AuctionWorks provides auction management services for eBay, Yahoo, and uBid. In addition to selling items on these auction sites, you can create your own online store on the AuctionWorks site. Services include inventory management, image hosting, customer database management, invoice and mailing label generation, billing and sales reporting, and merchant account setup. A couple of interesting features are the ability to change inventory, price, and shipping information fields for multiple inventory items, and LaunchBots™, an application for automatically setting up and maintaining scheduled, repeating auctions.

95. Register your own domain name

The problem with using free host sites or space on your Internet service provider's (ISP's) system is that you will probably end up with a long and hard-to-remember URL. The part of the URL before the period is called the domain name. The part after the period (i.e. ".com," ".net," ".org," etc.) is called the top-level domain name. The solution is to register your own domain name. It used to be that only one organization, InterNic, registered and maintained all the Internet domain names. However, today there are many online companies that provide this service including many ISPs.

In addition to registration, you might need a forwarding service. This depends on who is hosting your website. If you parked your website on a free host site or an ISP that does not provide a service to connect your registered domain name to where your site actually exists, then you will need a forwarding service. A forwarding service connects visitors to the actual location of your website and forwards e-mail addressed as your-name@your-name.com to wherever your actual e-mail is received. The charge for this service is usually a monthly or yearly maintenance fee.

You can have one service manage the registration of your domain name and another, separate service handle the forwarding. Most forwarding services will also register your domain name so you can have them do both if you want.

Resources

The following sites provide domain registration. Some also provide forwarding services.

NameSecure
http://www.NameSecure.com

Network Solutions
http://www.networksolutions.com

Register
http://www.register.com

Verisign
http://www.verisign.com

96. Make your website "search-engine friendly"

In addition to the basic information you submit to a search engine or registration service when you register your page, search engines compile information, such as keywords and abstracts, from the text information and

HTML tags contained in the site's individual Web pages. They do this by using special software called "spiders." You enhance the chances that a browser will find your site and that the search engine will provide meaningful information by embedding specific information in your website.

Here are some design tips to make your website search-engine friendly:

- Avoid symbols in your URL because many search engines do not recognize them.

- The search engines draw much of their information from the home page of your site. This is usually the first page a browser sees when visiting your site. Make sure you have text on your home page. Don't design a home page that contains graphics only. Besides taking longer to download, graphically intensive home pages don't provide enough text for a search engine to use.

- Place a summary paragraph at the top of each page describing page contents. Include keywords that browsers are likely to use in a search for your site and limit the summary to about 250 words or less.

- Keep in mind that each search engine has different methods of deciding what criteria are best for its engines. Therefore, it is a good idea to learn as much as you can about specific engines, so that you can target them.

- Refrain from registering your site with a search engine more than once. If you do this with some search engines, they lower your ranking in any search results list.

- Place descriptive keywords between the <TITLE> HTML tags on each page of your website.

- Use <META> HTML tags to provide additional description and keywords for search engines. For example, the <META> HTML code for a Web page description is:

  <META Name = "description" content = "Your page description">

  For keywords, the HTML code is:

  <META Name = "keywords" content = Keyword1, Keyword2, etc">

- Be creative when selecting keywords. Keep in mind not everyone thinks of the same words you do, especially for an international audience. For example, while we call a certain type of store a "drug store," the British call them "chemists." For this reason, you should try to include a wide range of keywords relevant to your site. You should even consider including commonly misspelled words because many people are not aware of the correct spelling. Include misspelled words only in hidden Web page information like <META> tags and not in any text displayed to the browser.

- Use the <ALT> HTML tag to describe your graphics. Because search engines cannot read graphics, this provides a text description the search engine can use.

Resources

Poor Richard's Internet Marketing and Promotions
by Peter Kent and Tara Calishain.
Lakewood, CO: Top Floor Publishing, 1999, ISBN 0-9661032-7-0.
This book is an outstanding resource covering marketing and promotions on the Internet. It includes tips on how to register your site, promote your e-newsletter, and use e-mail for marketing.

97. Register your website with search engines

You can register your website with the main search engines in two ways. You can either manually submit your registration to each search engine or use one of several registration services to do the job for you. Several registration services let you enter basic information about your site once and then submit this information to the search engines you select. Some registration services do this for free, while others charge a fee.

Keep in mind that most search engines have a waiting period before they list a page, ranging from a few minutes to a few weeks. Whether you register once with a registration service or multiple times with the different search engines, be prepared to provide some basic information about your site.

Although the required registration information varies with different search engines and registration services, the following is a list of common information most require:

- Your website's URL
- A list of keywords that describe your website
- A 35- to 50-word description of your website
- The name, e-mail address, and phone number of a contact person.

Resources

The following websites provide search engine registration services:

bCentral
http://www.bCentral.com

Site Meter
http://promo.sitemeter.com

A1 Communications
http://www.a1co.com

Did-it
http://www.did-it.com

98.   Pay for a sponsored link

While many of the major websites require a minimum $2,000 to $3,000 for premium placement, at least one site, google.com, provides a more economical alternative. With Google's AdWords program, you can create a sponsored link that appears on a topic appropriate Google search results page. How much do you pay for each click through? With Google, that depends on you. After you pay a $5 activation fee, you set how much you are willing to pay per click and per day. You can choose a maximum cost-per-click (CPC) from $0.05 to $50, and set a daily budget as low as 5 cents. There is no minimum monthly charge, and you only pay for people who click through to your site.

As for ad placement, Google AdWords does not rank ads solely on cost. There is no way to reserve the top placement in the AdWords program. Ad placement is based on a combination of your maximum CPC and click through rate (CTR). This means that if you earn a higher CTR, you are rewarded with a lower actual CPC and a higher position.

Resources

For more information see the Google AdWords home page at:
https://AdWords.google.com

99. Put your contact information on every page of your website

Make it easy for browsers to contact you, by putting your contact information on every page of your website rather than banishing it to your "Contact Us" page. Put this information at the top and bottom of each page. Decide what minimum contact information you want to include such as your phone number, fax number, and e-mail address. However, don't get rid of your "Contact Us" page because many website browsers look for this standard page for contact information.

100. Add content feeds to your website

If you want people to return to your website, you have to constantly update it with new content. This can be very time consuming, particularly for a small or one-person business with limited time. So how can you keep your website fresh with a minimum of upkeep? Use content feeds.

What are content feeds? They're web services that automatically feed your website with constantly updated content. Types of feeds include news, surveys, polls, message boards, cartoons, animated cursors, tickers, and counters.

Resources

Interest! Alert

http://www.interestalert.com

This site lets you put headlines and summaries on your website. When browsers click on a news link, they view the full story on the Interest! ALERT site. The affiliate program pays 0.0025 per paid view of the news pages it serves. You can make up to $50 per year, which you can apply to the other services.

MoreOver

http://www.moreover.com

MoreOver offers hundreds of pre-built public feeds across a range of topics. You use a data feed by pasting the HTML code provided into your website.

Sparklit

http://www.sparklit.com

This site offers free Web polls and other services such as surveys and online forms. If you want more sophisticated polls, you can sign up for the Gold Polls option, which includes advanced features, improved integration, and no advertising or Sparklit branding.

EZpolls

http://ezpolls.superstats.com

For $19.95 per month, EZpolls Professional offers customizable polls for your website.

101. Become an affiliate

Another way you can add content to your website and make some money is to become an affiliate. Affiliates are basically resellers of products and services over the Internet. There are literally thousands of affiliate programs, and major Internet retailers such as Amazon.com have affiliate programs. Anyone with a website can apply to become an affiliate. Once you are accepted, the retailer provides you with some prewritten HTML code to insert into a page on your website. The HTML code typically provides a graphic and a link to products on the retailer's website. When browsers click on the link in your website, they are transferred to the retailer's website, and if they buy anything, you receive compensation from the retailer. The retailer knows they came from your site based on a code embedded in the link from your site.

Affiliate compensation usually takes the form of a commission based on a percentage of any sales made to people who linked to the seller's site from your site. Many affiliate programs give you the option of getting your compensation in cash or in credit toward products on their site. Usually, if you opt for cash, you have to wait longer to get paid or wait until your balance rises to a particular level before you are compensated. If you take credit, you usually get to take your compensation more quickly and at a lower balance than if you opt for cash.

Because there are so many affiliate programs to choose from, it's not unusual to include several offerings from different sellers on your site. This increases the range of products you can offer on your site, but it also increases the hassle of separately tracking payments from several different affiliate programs. To solve this problem, some Internet companies offer the service of managing many affiliate commission programs under one account.

Resources

Commission Junction
http://www.cj.com
Earn additional income by hosting advertising banners on your website. Although this is not a new idea, Commission Junction adds a different tactic by centralizing payment for affiliate programs offered by companies like hotjobs.com and eBay. Rather than enter into affiliate programs for each vendor separately, you can select from Commission Junction's list of participating companies and receive payment for all the sales commissions from one source.

Affiliate Network
http://www.affiliatenetwork.com
The Affiliate Network is an International Affiliate Network. The site doesn't have as many merchants as Commission Junction, but the advantages of centralized payment are the same. It also offers the option of being paid via PayPal.

102. Participate in banner exchanges

Banner exchange services display banners for members of the network on member websites. Sometimes a portion of the banner space is sold to sponsors; this setup allows the exchange site to offer this service for free. If you participate in one of these programs, determine whether you can opt out of banners displayed for certain types of businesses that you may not want to advertise on your site.

In addition to formal banner exchange services, you can organize your own link exchanges by being listed in the links page of other websites. You can do this informally by contacting other complementary businesses and offering to provide a link to their website in exchange for a reciprocal link on your website. Check your list of vendors, customers, professional organizations, and websites of industry publications for possible sources of link exchanges.

Resources

Bannerswap

http://www.bannerswap.com

LinkTrader

http://www.linktrader.com

Marketing Through the Internet

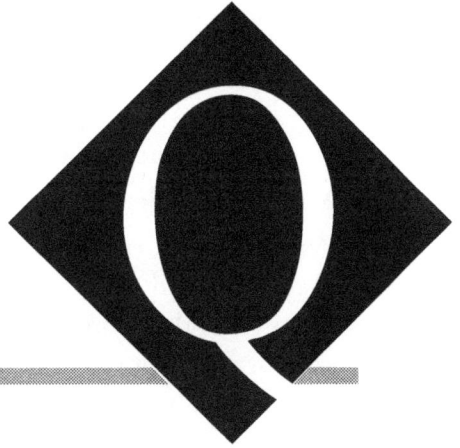

*"The Internet is like a giant jellyfish. You can't step on it.
You can't go around it. You've got to get through it."*
—John Evans

In addition to creating a website, there are many other ways to market on the Internet. The Internet has delivered a more level playing field to free agents to connect your message to a target audience at a significantly lower cost than traditional mass-marketing methods.

However, as with any marketing effort, you have to make an effort to find your target audience on the Internet and make it easy for them to find you. You can maximize your marketing message through your online communications by using e-mail signatures, auto responders, and messenger services. You can become a part of the Internet marketplace through job sites, online directories, and classified ads. You can research your target market by analyzing website guest books and participating in online discussion boards. Finally, you can use the Internet to get attention by offering valuable content through a webinar or online newsletter.

103. Use an e-mail signature

An e-mail signature is a small segment of text at the end of your e-mail messages. You can add this text manually or by using cut-and-paste, but most e-mail and contact software includes the capability to automatically insert an e-mail signature.

What should you put in your e-mail signature? Here are some suggestions:

* Your name and the name of your company
* The URL of your website
* Your phone number or the 800 number for orders
* Your e-mail address
* The e-mail address of an auto responder. An auto responder can automatically send an e-mail to anyone who sends a message to the auto-responder address. You can use this to provide an e-mail version of your brochure or to provide a free "ten tips" document to people interested in your business.

Here's an example of an e-mail signature:

———————————————————————————
DOUGLAS FLORZAK/Logical Directions, Inc.
dflorzak@LogicalDirections.com - www.LogicalDirections.com
AUTHOR OF "Successful Independent Consulting
 - Turn Your Career Experience Into a Consulting Business"
Phone orders: 1-800-431-1579
BOOK INFO: http://www.amazon.com/exec/obidos/ASIN/
0967156548/successfulindy
———————————————————————————

104. Use an auto responder

An auto responder is an e-mail address that automatically sends a pre-composed e-mail message to anyone who sends a message to the auto responder. The potential uses of this tool are endless. You can use auto-responders to provide text brochures, register people for your newsletter, provide free reports, or provide your rate schedule. Your ISP or Web page hosting service may already provide auto responder services. If not, there are numerous third-party auto responder services available on the Internet. You can also create your own auto responder by manipulating the filter features available with the major e-mail and contact software providers.

Resources

Autoresponder-Review.Com

http://www.autoresponder-review.com

This site strives to provide relevant and useful comparisons of auto responders. In each review it discusses the pros and cons of the service and provides pricing information. It also provides articles on maximizing results from auto responders.

105. Use an Internet messenger service

Internet messenger services provide a way to do real-time, remote networking. If you can get on your client's instant messenger service list, it's as close as you can come to having a permanent cubicle in the office. When a client with a new project and a short deadline notices that you're online, the company can do the electronic equivalent of sticking its head above the cubicle wall and asking whether you're available to help. This method of communication is quicker than e-mail and more efficient than a phone call.

Does your client use an instant messenger service? If the company doesn't use one, suggest that it adopt one for more efficient logistics between your businesses.

Resources

AOL Instant Messenger™

http://www.aim.com

MSN

http://www.messenger.msn.com

Yahoo

http://www.messenger.yahoo.com

106. Post your resume on job sites

There are literally hundreds of job boards ranging from the appropriately named monster.com to much smaller niche job boards. If you are an independent consultant, free-lancer, contractor, free agent, or other fee- or project-based business, you can search these job boards for potential work and/or post your resume to these sites. Posting your resume on most job sites is free, but some charge a fee in exchange for a promise of a more focused distribution of your resume.

Job and career sites break down into three general categories: big boards, geographically centered, and industry specific. Big boards such as monster.com, careerbuilder.com, and dice.com have the advantage of higher visibility, more jobs, and more traffic. However, they are also more generic and attract a great deal of competition for the same contract or position. Geographically centered and industry specific boards are smaller and more targeted, affording you a more focused marketing effort.

When you use a job site to market your business through your resume, don't overestimate the possible results. This is not a substitute for other forms of networking. The competition is tough. There might be hundreds or thousands of responses to a job posted on a job site, and don't forget this is the Internet. The potential competition includes the entire world. However, adding your information to several job site databases is relatively quick and inexpensive, so it can't hurt to participate.

Here are some things to keep in mind when submitting your resume to job sites:

- **Be clear about your employment status.** Unless you are looking for a full-time job as an employee of a company, make it clear somewhere in your resume that you are a free agent looking for a contract relationship.

- **Create a resume without fancy formatting.** For most of these sites, you will fill out structured forms or paste your resume information as simple text into one big form field. Thus, you should have a version of your resume that does not include tabs, bold, italic, or special fonts.

- **Include a list of keywords at the bottom of your resume.** It's rare that a real person reviews a resume submitted online. Most companies use electronic screening programs to scan for keywords. You can increase the chance of a "hit" if you include relevant keywords as part of your resume.

- **Review your information before you save it.** Spell-check your information off-line before you copy it to paste on a job site. Make sure that the information you paste to the job-site field doesn't have any odd line breaks.

- **Watch out for scammers.** The media has reported some instances in which fake jobs have been posted to collect personal information that can be used for identity theft. Do not put your Social Security number in your resume or profile information. Typically, you should not have to supply your social security number to a client until you start working for them and they need this information for your Form 1099.

Resources

Contract Job Hunter

http://www.cjhunter.com

A service of the C.E. Weekly newsletter, this site provides information about job openings for contractors and consultants in engineering, IT/IS, and technical disciplines. For a small yearly fee, members enjoy services such as online resume, e-mail resume distribution, hot sheet listing, message boards, online directory of contract staffing firms, articles, editorials, and columns. One nice feature of the search engine is that the results highlight your search words.

Data Processing Independent Consultants Exchange (DICE)

http://www.dice.com

Originally designed primarily for independent consultants in the IT industry, Dice now includes permanent as well as contract jobs. Most listings are by agencies representing clients.

Elance.com

http://www.elance.com

For a monthly fee, this job site provides billing and payment services that facilitate international transactions. You can also bid on projects at this site.

FedBizOpps

http://www.fedbizopps.gov

FedBizOpps provides a single point of entry for Federal Government procurement opportunities over $25,000. Government buyers can publicize their business opportunities by posting information directly to FedBizOpps via the Internet. Through one portal, commercial vendors seeking federal markets for their products and services can search, monitor, and retrieve opportunities solicited by the entire federal contracting community.

FreeAgent.com

http://www.FreeAgent.com

This site provides an employment service called Yurcor, where the contractor works for Yurcor, which acts as an umbrella employer providing benefits and business tax deductions.

FreelanceWriters.com

http://www.freelancewriters.com

This site maintains a database of freelance writers worldwide. A small annual fee entitles you to a 300-word biography, a link to your website, and an e-mail address. The registration includes an extensive list of categories to which you can relate your writing skills.

Home Job Stop

http://homejobstop.com

This site's job bank includes a diverse database of telecommuting (work-at-home) jobs in a variety of disciplines available locally, nationally, and worldwide. You can access the database for a small one-time fee. There is a nominal one-time fee to post your resume on the site. They also charge a small yearly subscription fee to receive biweekly reports of the newest job listings, mailed directly to your e-mail.

Monster Contract & Temporary Community

http://talentmarket.monster.com

This part of the Monster board is built specifically for contractors and free agents. You can submit your resume to be part of the Monster database. The C&T Community website includes a search function customized for contract and temporary workers as well as articles, message boards, and a chat area.

107. List your business in online directories

There are many opportunities to be listed in online business directories. These are different from search engine listings because searches can be based on specific fields of information. These types of directories can range from generic directories, such as the traditional paper yellow pages, to very industry-specific listings. Some are free and others charge for a listing.

With the generic sites, you are a little fish in a big pond. You might get lost in noise because so many other businesses are competing for attention. However, these sites also tend to generate more traffic than industry-specific websites. When you are listed in an industry- specific site, you are a little fish in a small pond. Your chance of being seen is greater, but traffic to the site may be lower than that on a generic site. If possible, you can maximize your chances by being listed in both types of sites (generic and industry specific).

Resources

Switchboard.com

http://www.Switchboard.com

If you're listed in any local business yellow pages listings, you may already be listed on this site. For additional fees, you can add a directory listing that links to your existing website, an enhanced listing that links directly to your website and promotes additional information about your business, an online "coupon" (direct link to promote your special offer), and a one- or two-page website.

PayPal

http://www.PayPal.com

Anyone who regularly purchases items on eBay is familiar with PayPal. In addition to using PayPal to handle payments and credit transactions with your business, you can be listed in the PayPal Shops directory as one of the businesses that accepts PayPal.

108. Place an online classified ad

Another way to publicize your website is to list it on Internet classified websites. Most of these sites offer some sort of free ad service. Usually for additional fees, you can display more lines of text or even one Web page.

Resources

InterMall
http://www.1mall.com

BestAds
http://www.bestads.com

Epages
http://www.ep.com

NetBistro
http://www.netbistro.com

109. Participate in online groups

Online forums in the form of news groups, bulletin boards, discussion groups, and community websites serve as the Internet's meeting rooms. You can use online forums passively or actively. When you use online forums passively for research, you read but don't submit your own response (this is known as "lurking"). By periodically checking the discussion threads of forums appropriate to your business, you may detect a trend or niche that you can serve.

When you participate actively in an online forum, you maintain a higher profile. To do this properly, you have to take the position that you are a resource for the group and not someone who is trying to exploit the group's list to sell your wares. Here are some ways you can productively work with an online group:

• **Submit articles.** Write a "ten tips" related to your service or product.

• **Answer questions.** If someone in the group submits a question in your area of expertise, respond with an answer.

• **Ask a question.** Ask a question of your own or start a discussion about an issue relevant to your industry.

- **Provide resources.** If you come across a website, article, or product (other than your own) that you think the group will appreciate, submit it.

In each of these types of messages, it is acceptable to include your contact information and website address at the end of the article with a brief description of your business.

Resources

Google Groups (formerly deja.com)

http://groups.google.com

This list of news groups includes a tool for searching for groups based on keywords. When it displays a list of groups, a gauge indicates how active the group is.

Yahoo Groups

http://groups.yahoo.com

In addition to standard group messages, Yahoo Groups includes the ability to upload files, photos, links, and tables. It also includes a chat area for live typed conversations, an area where you can offer a group poll, and a calendar.

Meetup.com

http://www.meetup.com

This group goes a step further than the typical online group. The website organizes people who participate in groups into geographic areas based on zip code and partners with local restaurants and bars to schedule in-person group meetings.

110. View guest books

Many websites include a "guest book" in which browsers can enter their name, e-mail address, and comments about the website. By viewing the guest books of websites relevant to your business, you can gain an idea of the type of people who are visiting these sites. Sometimes this information also includes the e-mail address of the guest.

Visit the websites of your competitors, vendors, and clients to determine whether they have a guest book. In some cases, you might be able to make an entry in a guest book and mention your site.

111. Create an online newsletter

Online newsletters have many advantages. Compared to paper newsletters, they are inexpensive to produce and distribute. However, like their paper counterparts, online newsletters demand an investment of time.

The purpose of an online newsletter is to provide some valuable content to clients and potential clients. Your newsletter should not be a brochure in disguise. Avoid blatant slogans and sales pitches. By providing a valuable resource to your readers, you will capture their attention long enough to think about your company.

The four major issues regarding an online newsletter concern content, frequency, method of distribution, and administration.

1. **Content.** How do you find subjects to write about in your newsletter? People typically read paper or online newsletters because they provide tips, how-to information, or industry scuttlebutt that helps them solve a problem or problems. Here are some ideas:

   - Write about ways you or your company solved recent client problems
   - Provide a tip about how to use a piece of software more efficiently for a client in your industry
   - Review books relevant to your industry
   - Reference recent stories that appeared in industry trade papers.

2. **Frequency.** How often do you intend to publish your electronic newsletter? Common choices are daily, biweekly, monthly, bimonthly, quarterly, and annually. You can pick any frequency you want provided you can make a commitment to meet the deadline you imposed on yourself. The trick is to find a frequency that doesn't demand too much of your time but puts your newsletter in front of your subscribers often enough to keep you fresh in their minds.

3. **Method of distribution.** After you've pulled your content together and decided how often you'll publish, you have to select a method for distributing your newsletter. There are three ways to distribute your newsletter: self-distribute, use a free service, or pay for a service.

   The advantage of self-distribution is that it costs nothing and you control the entire content of the newsletter. The disadvantage is that you have to invest more time administering your distribution list. The advantage of a "free" service is that it takes care of most of the administrative tasks, but the "price" for this service is the right of the service to insert random advertisements into your newsletter. However, you usually can exclude any advertisements that you think your readers would find offensive or inappropriate, such as advertisements for adult websites, religious organizations, and alcohol or tobacco ads. When you pay for a service to distribute your newsletter, you avoid random ads and the service takes care of the administration, but you have to pay a monthly fee for something you are likely distributing for free.

4. **Administration.** Regardless of the distribution method, you have to control three administrative tasks when you publish an electronic newsletter adding new subscribers, removing nonsubscribers, and dealing with messages bounced due to bad e-mail addresses. The newsletter services can automate most of these activities. If you're self-distributing your newsletter, some e-mail programs such as Eudora and Outlook can automate some of these processes through their rules feature, but you may still have some manual tasks.

Resources

Topica
http://www.topica.com
Topica provides a free service for maintaining an e-mail list for your newsletter. People you add to the list must opt in before they receive your mailings. To opt in, the recipient responds to an invitation sent through Topica.

Constant Contact
http://www.ConstantContact.com
Constant Contact provides easy to use templates for an online newsletter. The price of the service is based on the number of recipients in your mailing list. If your list is less than 50 recipients, you can use the service for free. After you send a newsletter (Constant Contact calls this a "campaign"), the service provides statistics measuring bad e-mail addresses and click-throughs for links in the newsletter.

112. Conduct a "webinar"

One step beyond a telephone seminar is a webinar. A webinar is a combination telephone and Web browser seminar. Similar to a telephone seminar, participants call into a conference coordinator to hear the audio of the presentation. At the same time, they connect to a website that displays the presenter's slides. The slide presentation is synchronized and controlled by the presenter as if the presenter was in the same room with the participants. Some seminar hosting services also offer the capability to share applications for training and display an electronic "wipe board," on which the presenter can manually draw, write, and annotate items in the display area just like a physical wipe board.

As with telephone seminars, there are webinar service providers. They usually charge a flat monthly fee or per person for single events. If your information is valuable enough, you might be able to charge at least enough to cover your costs.

The disadvantage of some webinar hosts is that for the participants to get the full benefit of the presentation, they sometimes need two connections; a telephone connection for the audio and an internet connection through another telephone line, DSL, cable modem, or other means. If you are addressing a business audience, this probably isn't an issue because most businesses have at least two phone lines. But if you're addressing a consumer audience or an audience in remote locations with limited Internet access, you might want to present a telephone seminar.

Resources

Interwise

http://www.interwise.com
800-598-8004

Interwise provides e-learning hosting services for seminars, online meetings, mentoring, and broadcasts. Their hosting software can transmit both audio and visual elements of a presentation through the Internet, so participants do not have to have two connections.

PlaceWare

http://www.placeware.com

This Microsoft subsidiary has the technology to host live online training and conferences with 2 to 2500 remote attendees. Attendees can participate by using only a Web browser and a telephone.

Present Online

http://www.presentonline.com

877-210-3630

Present Online provides a platform for interactive presentations including one-to-one meetings, internal conferences, team meetings, and/or public seminars. The tools allow you to broadcast Microsoft PowerPoint® slides, in real time, directly from your desktop through the website to logged-on participants. Participants can also hear the audio of your broadcast on their phone by dialing a toll-free number. Additional features are the chat and polling functions, universal whiteboard, and record/playback of archived presentations.

Bibliography

Florzak, Douglas. *Successful Independent Consulting: Turn Your Career Experience into a Consulting Business.* Westmont, IL: Logical Directions, Inc., 1999.

Godin, Seth. *Purple Cow: Transform Your Business by Being Remarkable.* Dobbs Ferry, NY: Portfolio, 2003.

Holtz, Herman. *How to Succeed as an Independent Consultant.* New York: John Wiley & Sons, 1988.

Kent, Peter & Tara Calishain. *Poor Richard's Internet Marketing and Promotions: How to Promote Yourself, Your Business, Your Ideas Online.* Lakewood, CO: Top Floor Publishing, 1999.

Kintler, David. *Independent Consulting.* Avon, MA: Adams Media Corporation, 1998.

Levinson, Jay Conrad. *Guerrilla Marketing Weapons: 100 Affordable Marketing Methods for Maximizing Profits from Your Small Business.* New York: Penguin Group, 1990.

Lonier, Terri. *Working Solo*, 2nd ed. New York: John Wiley & Sons, Inc., 1998.

Michaels, Nancy & Debbi J. Karpowicz. *Off-the-Wall Marketing Ideas.* Avon, MA: Adams Media Corporation, 2000.

National Business Employment Weekly. *Networking.* New York: John Wiley & Sons, 1994.

Pink, Daniel H. *Free Agent Nation.* New York, Warner Books, 2001.

Ruhl, Janet. *The Computer Consultant's Guide.* New York: John Wiley & Sons, 1994.

Shenson, Howard L. *The Contract and Fee-Setting Guide for Consultants & Professionals.* New York: John Wiley & Sons, 1990.

Weiss, Alan. *Million Dollar Consulting: The Professional's Guide to Growing a Practice*, 3rd ed. New York: McGraw-Hill, 2003.

Index

R$_x$ for Layoffs!

Successful Independent Consulting

Turn Your Career Experience Into a Consulting Business

by Doug Florzak

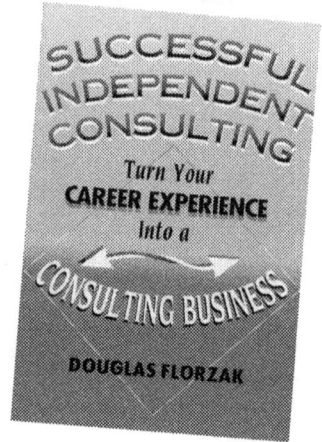

Consult Your Way to a New Career!

Whether you are already a consultant or thinking about becoming one, this guide shows you how to:

- Start your own consulting business
- Set up a website and find Web resources
- Implement Internet marketing strategies
- Create a business plan
- Set your rate structure

- Understand incorporation and tax issues
- Set up your home office
- Set up retirement funding
- Understand basic record-keeping
- Select appropriate insurance

The book also includes a recommended resource list and sample worksheets to help you start and maintain your consulting business. This is a life-changing book for experienced professionals at a crossroads in their career. Declare your independence! Successful Independent Consulting is a must for those contemplating self-employment.

Here's what reviewers are saying:

"Successful Independent Consulting is not a book bogged down with legal terms or financial script, but communicates necessary information in a refreshingly quick and to-the-point manner."

—ForeWord Magazine

"For readers who are dying to go into the consulting biz (you have just been fired or are overworked or disillusioned), Florzak provides a wealth of information on getting started in this new field."

—American Library Association *Booklist*

"If you want to be a consultant but don't know anything about setting up or running your own business, or are thinking about becoming a consultant, this book can help and let you turn your career experience into a consulting business."   —About.com

This book is available from your local bookseller, online supplier, or use the order form on the next page ❯

Give the Gift of
The Free Agent Marketing Guide
to Your Friends and Colleagues

☐ Please send me _____ copies of *The Free Agent Marketing Guide* at $18.95 each for a total of $_____

☐ Please send me _____ copies of *Successful Independent Consulting: Turn Your Career Experience into a Consulting Business* at $17.95 each for a total of $_____

☐ Please send me _____ e-Book CD copies in Adobe Acrobat PDF of *Successful Independent Consulting* at $8.95 each for a total of $_____

◆ Add $4.90 shipping for the first item $ 4.90

◆ Add $1.00 shipping each additional item after the first $_____

SUBTOTAL: $_____

◆ Illinois residents, please add 6.75% (0.0675) sales tax $_____

TOTAL: $_____

Note: All amounts are in US dollars. Canadian orders must be accompanied by a postal money order in U.S. funds. Allow 15 days for delivery. Volume discounts available for orders of 5 or more books; contact the publisher for details via address below or email book@LogicalDirections.com.

Payment Method: ☐ enclosed check or money order   ☐ Visa   ☐ MasterCard

Name _____

Organization _____

Address _____

City/State/Zip _____

Phone _____

eMail _____

Card # _____ Exp. Date _____

Signature _____

☐ YES, I am interested in having Doug Florzak speak or give a seminar to my company, association, school, or organization. Please send information.

Please make your check payable and return to:
Logical Directions, Inc., PO Box 19, Westmont, IL 60559

Call your credit card order to 800-431-1579 (books only)
Fax your order to: 708-575-2899
Order online: www.LDIPub.com

Free CD!
The Free Agent Marketing Guide
Resources CD

As a "thank you" for purchasing this book, we are offering you a free copy of the *Free Agent Resources CD*. This CD includes an Adobe Acrobat PDF document with all the resources mentioned in the book plus many additional resources that didn't make it into publication. The resource listings include live links to the websites mentioned in the book. The CD also includes a recording of a radio interview with the author, Doug Florzak.

☐ YES, send me my FREE copy of *The Free Agent Marketing Guide* Resource CD. I've included $4.90 for shipping. Canadian orders must be accompanied by a postal money order in U.S. funds for shipping. Allow 15 days for delivery.

☐ My check or money order for **$4.90** to cover shipping is enclosed.
Please charge my ☐ Visa ☐ MasterCard

Name _____

Organization _____

Address _____

City/State/Zip _____

Phone _____

eMail _____

Outlet where you bought this book _____

Card #_____ Exp. Date _____

Signature _____

Note: this offer is only available directly from the publisher. Only one CD per address.
Please make your check payable and return to:
Logical Directions, Inc.
PO Box 19, Westmont, IL 60559
Fax your order to: 708-575-2899

About the Author:

Doug Florzak is a Certified Guerrilla Marketing Coach. He's been interviewed by the *Chicago Tribune*, The *New York Times*, and *Crain's Chicago Business* for his advice on independent consulting. He's also a contributor to *Contract Professional* magazine. Doug's consulting experience includes many years as a systems technology consultant for GTE Telenet and Wang Laboratories, and over a decade as an independent consultant. He is founder of Logical Directions, Inc., a communications firm specializing in training development and technical and business communications. Doug is also an Associate Fellow of the Society for Technical Communication (STC) where he's won several awards for document design.

How to Contact the Author:

Doug Florzak is available to the media for interviews and as a speaker for your company, association, sales organization, or chamber of commerce. He speaks about guerrilla marketing, starting a business as an independent consultant, and getting published. To discuss hiring him for your next meeting, conference, fund-raiser, or special event, contact:

Douglas Florzak
Logical Directions, Inc.
P.O. Box 19
Westmont, IL 60559
Phone: **708-575-2899**
E-mail: **dflorzak@LDIPub.com**

Attention Corporations, Associations, Universities, Colleges, and Sales Organizations:

Bulk Discounts

Discounts start at only 10 copies. Save from 20% to 55% off retail price.

Custom Publishing

We can custom publish a cover with your organization's name and logo and develop custom booklets or pamphlets from our books.

Supplemental Materials

We can develop workshop outlines, training materials, classroom tools, and other resources based on our books.

For information, please contact Logical Directions, Inc., PO Box 19, Westmont, IL 60559. E-mail publisher@LDIPub.com.

www.ingramcontent.com/pod-product-compliance
Lightning Source LLC
Chambersburg PA
CBHW032100080426
42733CB00006B/349